Piano • Vocal • Guitar

Alan Menken SONGBOOK

Cover Photo: Dave Cross: Dave Cross Photography

ISBN 0-634-04540-7

7777 W. Bluemound Rd. P.O. Box 13819 Milwaukee, WI 53213

In Australia Contact:
Hal Leonard Australia Pty. Ltd.
22 Taunton Drive P.O. Box 5130, Cheltenham East, 3192, Victoria, Australia
Email: ausadmin@halleonard.com

Visit Hal Leonard Online at
www.halleonard.com

Photo by Dave Cross:
Dave Cross Photography

ALAN MENKEN

Alan Menken was born in New York City on July 22, 1949. His family moved to New Rochelle in 1951 and Alan attended New Rochelle public schools until graduating high school in 1967. The Menken household was filled with music; Alan's mother (an actress) and father (the original "musical dentist") passed on to their children a passionate love of the Broadway Musical. Although growing playing piano and violin, in the sixties Alan began playing guitar joined some bands and developed a passionate interest in Rock and Roll, R & B, Folk, World Music and Jazz.

In 1967, thinking he'd follow in his father's footsteps as a dentist, he enrolled at NYU as a pre-Med. In 1971, he graduated with a degree in music. In 1970, while still at NYU, Alan was accepted as a composer/lyricist into the BMI Musical Theatre workshop. There he found his "greatest teacher" in Lehman Engel. A legendary Broadway conductor who studied musicals from the perspective of the Orchestra pit, Lehman taught composers and lyricists the craft of theatrical songwriting. From 1971 to 1985, Alan composed and showcased *Conversations with Pierre*, *Dear Worthy Editor*, *Apartment House* (with lyrics by Muriel Robinson), *Midnight*, *Harry the Rat* and *The Messiah on Mott Street* (with lyrics by David Spencer). In November 1972, Alan married Janis Roswick, a ballet dancer who performed in his Rock Ballet, *Children of the World*.

Alan's first produced musical was *God Bless You Mr. Rosewater*, with book and lyrics by Howard Ashman, adapted from the Kurt Vonnegut novel of the same name. Produced in the spring of 1979 at the WPA Theater, it received very encouraging reviews which led to a move to The Entermedia Theater on 2nd Avenue. Alan's next show was a revue, *Patch Patch Patch,* produced at The West Bank Café in the Summer of 1979.

In 1980, he worked on two musical projects: *Real Life Funnies* and *Atina: Evil Queen of the Galaxy*. *Real Life Funnies*, a revue based on Stan Mack's Village Voice comic strip, had music and lyrics by Alan and adaptation and direction by Howard Ashman. *Atina: Evil Queen of the Galaxy*, with book and lyrics by Steve Brown, was produced in workshop by Michael Bennett and directed by Tom O'Horgan under the title *Battle of the Giants*.

Alan and Howard Ashman took what they learned from *Rosewater* and applied those lessons to a little Off-Broadway musical about a man-eating plant. *Little Shop of Horrors* opened at the WPA Theater in the spring of '82 and moved immediately to the Orpheum Theater on 2nd Avenue, where it ran for over five years and established itself as the highest grossing Off-Broadway show ever. It won the New York Drama Critics Award and the Drama Desk Award for best musical, plus the Outer Critics Award, a London's Evening Standard Award and a Grammy nomination for Best Cast Album.

Following the success of *Little Shop*, Alan began a number of new projects. *The Thorn,* another project with book and lyrics by Steve Brown, was completed but never produced, due to Mr. Brown's death from AIDS in the Spring of 1983. *Honeymooners*, for which Alan wrote both music and lyrics, was never produced due to rights problems. A musical project with playwright/lyricist Tom Eyen, *Kicks: The Showgirl Musical*, went through three workshops but stopped short of production in 1984. Attempts to mount productions continued until Tom Eyen succumbed to AIDS in 1991.

Alan Menken with Stephen Schwartz on Pocahontas.
[Disney photo by Mike Ansell]

The highlights of those years were the birth of Alan and Janis' first child, a daughter named Anna, in April of 1985 and their purchase of a farm in Pennsylvania. Then came the film adaptation of *Little Shop of Horrors*, which reunited Alan and Howard Ashman. Plus, in the fall of 1987 they began work on the Disney animated feature, *The Little Mermaid*. When the film of *Little Shop* was released, it resulted in Alan's first Academy Award nomination, for the song "Mean Green Mother from Outer Space."

In the spring of '87, Alan and lyricist David Spencer's adaptation of *The Apprenticeship of Duddy Kravitz* was produced in Philadelphia. Based on the novel by Mordechai Richler, it was directed by Austin Pendleton with book by Mr. Pendleton and Mr. Richler.

As Alan was working on what would become his first major film song score, he and Janis were again blessed by the birth of their second daughter Nora in August of 1988. A move to upstate New York followed that fall. With Howard Ashman's encouragement, Alan decided to take on his first film scoring job, composing the dramatic underscore for *The Little Mermaid.* In 1990, Alan won two Academy Awards (Best Song to "Under the Sea"), two Golden Globes, two Grammy Awards and three BMI Awards for his songs and score to *The Little Mermaid*. At the same time, as he and Howard Ashman were beginning work on *Beauty and the Beast*, Alan found out that Howard was seriously ill from AIDS-related causes.

As Alan and Howard Ashman were completing their songs for *Beauty* and *Aladdin*, Alan wrote music and lyrics to "Measure of a Man", the theme song for *Rocky*, recorded by Elton John. He also collaborated with lyricist Jack Feldman on the score to *Newsies* and songs for the TV musical, *Polly.* In March of 1991, as Alan was preparing to leave for Hollywood to produce the song sessions for *Newsies,* Howard Ashman passed away. Later that year *Beauty and the Beast* was released to unanimous praise. It became the first animated film to be nominated for the Best Picture Academy Award. It earned Alan two Academy Awards and two Golden Globes for Best Score and Best Song ("Beauty and the Beast"), five BMI Awards, a Christopher Award, three Grammy Awards and another multi-platinum soundtrack album.

After Howard Ashman's passing, story changes on *Aladdin* necessitated major changes in the song score. Tim Rice joined with Alan to write the new song moments. In '92, their collaboration resulted in an Academy Award and a Golden Globe for Best Song ("A Whole New World") and another Best Score Oscar and Golden Globe as well as four Grammys. Perhaps the biggest thrill was achieving *Billboard's* #1 for the single of "A Whole New World" as well as the Grammy for Best Song of the Year.

Alan Menken with Sir Tim Rice on Aladdin. *[Disney photo by Robert Isenberg]*

Alan Menken with Howard Ashman. [Disney photo by Marcia Reed]

That same year, Alan also composed the score for the ABC/Kunhardt Productions miniseries *Lincoln,* and the music, along with lyrics by David Spencer, for the Off-Broadway musical *Weird Romance.* The following year, Alan's score to *Life with Mikey* included new songs with Jack Feldman and Stephen Schwartz.

For the 1995 Disney animated feature, *Pocahontas,* Alan's collaboration with lyricist Stephen Schwartz produced two Academy Awards, a Golden Globe and a Grammy. The Oscar-winning song, "Colors of the Wind", remained high on the *Billboard* charts for 20 weeks and the album of *Pocahontas* reached number one on the *Billboard* charts.

In April 1994, the Broadway stage version of *Beauty and the Beast* opened at The Palace Theater and became an immediate smash hit. As of this date, it is the 10th longest running show in Broadway history. Also, in December 1994, *A Christmas Carol* premiered at the Theater at Madison Square Garden, with lyrics by Lynn Ahrens, direction by Michael Ockrent and choreography by Susan Stroman. The 2002 Holiday season will mark its 9th year running.

In 1996, Disney released another Alan Menken / Stephen Schwartz collaboration, *The Hunchback of Notre Dame,* for which Alan composed the music to the songs and score. It received an Academy Award nomination for Best Score.

Alan Menken and Danny Troob in the studio. [Disney photo by Marcia Reed]

In 1997, a concert version of Alan Menken and Tim Rice's *King David* was the premiere production at the New Amsterdam Theatre. That same year, Alan's next animated project *Hercules*, with lyrics by David Zippel, was released by Disney. "Go the Distance", from that movie, received an Oscar nomination for best song.

In the spring of 1999, a stage adaptation of *Hunchback* opened in Berlin, Germany, with additional songs by Alan and Stephen Schwartz and book and direction by James Lapine. *Der Glockner von Notre Dame* closed in the spring of 2002 and was the longest running musical ever in Berlin.

In 2000, Alan's alma mater, NYU, presented him with a Doctor of Fine Arts degree.

As Alan's relationship with Disney Animation continues with his score to the upcoming animated Western, *Home on the Range* (with lyrics by Glenn Slater), his focus has been primarily theatrical. Alan and Glenn Slater are writing new songs to complete a stage adaptation of *The Little Mermaid.* Alan, lyricist Marion Adler, and book writer/director Connie Grappo are developing *The Ballad of Little Pinks*, a musical of the Damon Runyon short story, *Little Pinks.* Along with playwright Larry Gelbart and lyricist David Zippel, he's writing two new musicals; *Buzz*, based on the life of Busby Berkeley and *Lysistrata: Sex and the City-State.* Work continues on *The Apprenticeship of Duddy Kravitz* and *Kicks.* And Alan and Tim Rice are preparing *King David* for future stage production.

And never one to limit himself, Alan Menken and Alice Cooper have collaborated on a new recording/stage project; *Alice Cooper's Deadly Seven.*

Not yet underway but planned are stage adaptations of *The Idolmaker*, with lyrics by Glenn Slater and book by Rupert Holmes; *Leap of Faith*, with lyrics by Marion Adler and book by Janus Cercone; and *Newsies* for the stage.

BEAUTY AND THE BEAST

from Walt Disney's BEAUTY AND THE BEAST

Lyrics by HOWARD ASHMAN
Music by ALAN MENKEN

D(add9)
F♯m
Bare - ly e - ven friends, then some - bod - y
G(add9)
G/A
A7sus
A7
D(add9)
bends un - ex - pect - ed - ly. Just a lit - tle
A7sus
G/A
A7
D(add9)
D
Am7
D7
change. Small, to say the least. Both a lit - tle
G(add9)
Gmaj7
F♯m7
Em7
G/A
A7
scared, nei - ther one pre - pared, Beau - ty and the
rall.

D
A7sus
D(add9)
2 fr
Beast.
a tempo, tenderly
A7sus
F♯m
G(add9)
Ev - er just the same.
Ev - er a sur -
F♯m
G(add9)
F♯m7
prise.
Ev - er as be - fore,
ev - er just as
Bm
Bm7
2 fr
C
D
E
sure
as the sun will
rise.
Tale as old as
mf

B7sus
B7
E
B7sus
B7
time,
tune as old as
song.
E
G♯m
Bit - ter - sweet and
strange,
find - ing you can
A
B7sus
B7
E(add9)
change,
learn - ing you were wrong.
Cer - tain as the
dim.
B7sus
B7
E(add9)
E
Bm7
E7
sun
ris - ing in the
East,
tale as old as

A Amaj7 G♯m7 F♯m7 B7sus B7
4 fr
time, song as old as rhyme, Beau - ty and the
E B/D♯ C♯m E/B A Amaj7 G♯m7
Beast. Tale as old as time, song as old as
mp
dim.
p
rall.
F♯m7 B7sus B7 E(add9) Esus B B9
rhyme, Beau - ty and the Beast.
8va
loco
a tempo
E(add9) E
8va
molto rall.
8vb

A CHANGE IN ME

from Walt Disney's BEAUTY AND THE BEAST: THE BROADWAY MUSICAL

Words by TIM RICE
Music by ALAN MENKEN

To Coda
G6
D/A
A7sus
A7
D
G
Asus
A
I still de - pend u - pon
had dis - ap - peared for good.
For now I re - a - lize
F♯
F♯7/B
Dmaj7/A
G
D/F♯
that good can come from bad
That may not make me wise
Em7
A7sus
A7
D
Gsus2/E
but oh it makes me glad And I
D/F♯
G(add2)
G/A
D
Em7
Dmaj7/F♯
I nev - er thought I'd leave be - hind

G6
Em
A7sus
A7
D
my child - hood dreams but I don't mind
Em7
A7/E
D/F♯
G(add9)
G/A
For now I love the world I
D.C. al Coda
(take 2nd ending)
Bm
F♯m/A
D/A
Em/G
B/F♯
Em7
G(add2)/A
see
No change of heart A change in
CODA
F
B♭
Csus
C
But in its place I feel

A
Dm
Dm/C
B♭
Fsus2/A
F/A
a tru - er life be - gin
And it's so good and real
Gm7(add4)
Gm7
C7sus
C7
F
Gm7
Gm6
It must come from with - in and I
Am7
F/A
B♭
B♭/C
F
C7sus
F/A
I nev - er thought I'd leave be - hind
B♭maj7
B♭6
Gm7
C7sus
C7
F
Gm7
Gm6
my child - hood dreams but I don't mind

F/A
B♭(add2)
B♭/C
Dm
Am/C
F/C
I'm where and who I want to be
Gm/B♭
D/A
Gm7
C7sus
F
Gm7
F/A
B♭
C
No change of heart A change in me
sub. p
F
B♭
Csus
C
Dm
Slowly
Gm7
No change of heart A
rit.
Csus
C
F
Gm7
F/A
B♭
C
F
change in me.

COLD ENOUGH TO SNOW

Music by ALAN MENKEN
Lyrics by STEPHEN SCHWARTZ

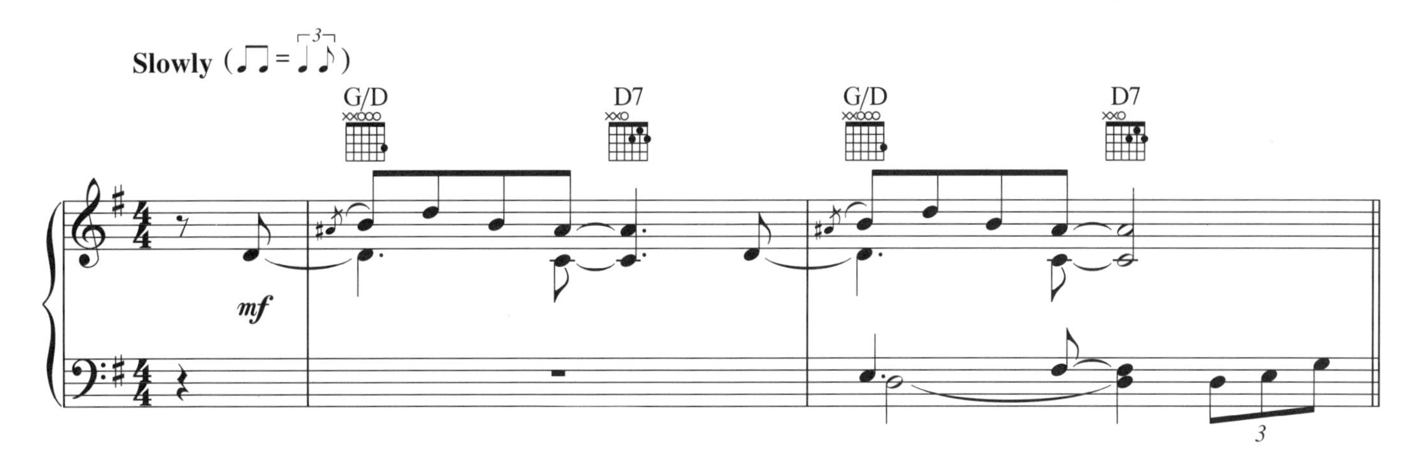

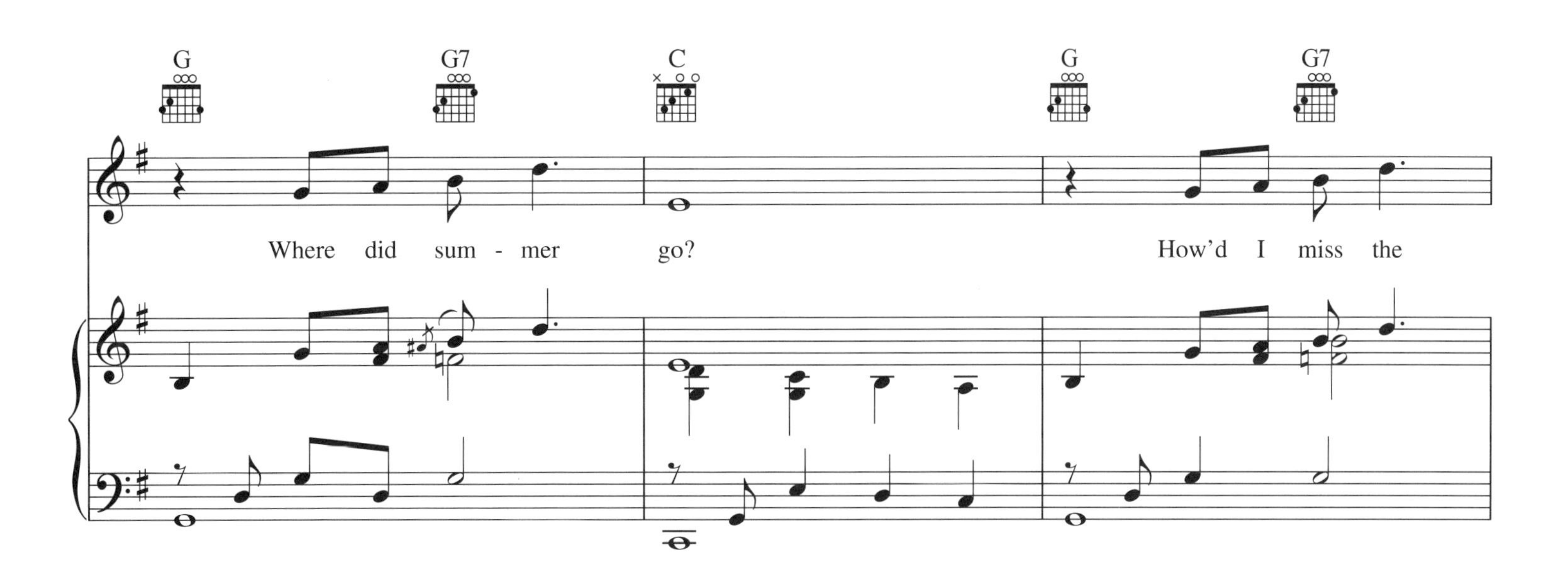

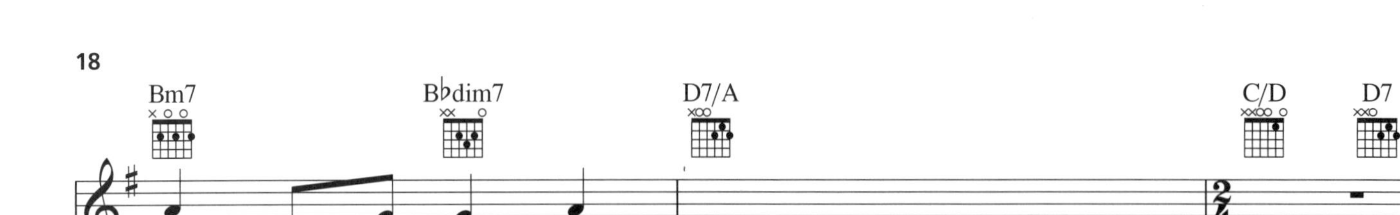
Bm7
B♭dim7
D7/A
C/D
D7

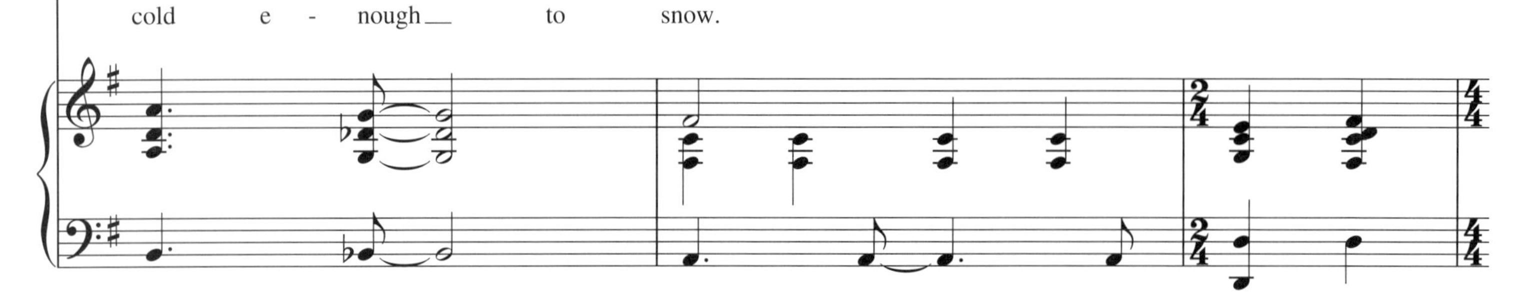
cold e - nough to snow.

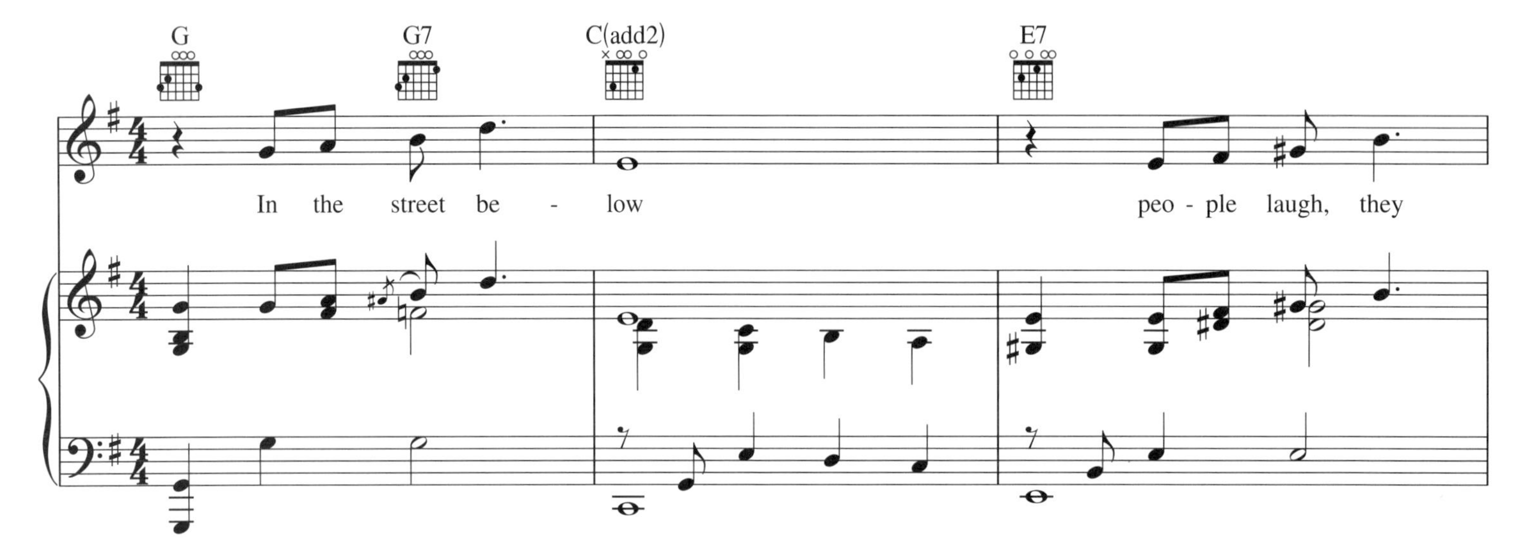
G
G7
C(add2)
E7
In the street be - low
peo - ple laugh, they

Am9
Cm6
Bm7
B♭dim7
Am9
D7sus
D7
got no rea - son. Don't they know it's cold e - nough to

G
C/G
G
Bm
snow?
When we were to - geth -

C(add2) Cm G/B D7/A G(add2) G
er and you were stay - in', fun - ny, but the
F♯m7♭5 B7 Em Em/D A9sus A7
weath - er still felt like May in
C/D D7 C/D D7 G G7 C(add2)
mid - De - cem - ber. Now the chill winds blow;
E Am9 Cm6 Bm7 B♭dim7
sun - ny skies, they're on - ly teas - in'. You won't show, and it's

Am7
Csus2/D
D7
G
Bm
cold e - nough to snow.
When we were to - geth -
C(add2)
C
G/B
D7/A
G(add2)
F♯m11
B7
er and you were stay - in'; fun - ny, but the weath -
Em
G/A
A7
D7sus
D7
C/D
F7
er still felt like May in mid - De - cem - ber.
B♭
B♭7
E♭
G
G7
On the ra - di - o there's a guy says

Cm(add2)
E♭m6
Dm7
D♭dim
4fr
Cm7
E♭/F
D/F♯
it ain't freez - in'. What's he know? He did - n't watch you
Gm
E♭maj9
B♭sus2/D
go. Now the sun can shine. If it
rit.
Cm7
3fr
Dm7
G7
Cm11
F7sus
F7
wants to, fine, but it's cold e - nough to
B♭
B♭7
E♭6/B♭
E♭m/B♭
6fr
B♭
snow.
a tempo
L.H.

COLORS OF THE WIND

from Walt Disney's POCAHONTAS

Music by ALAN MENKEN
Lyrics by STEPHEN SCHWARTZ

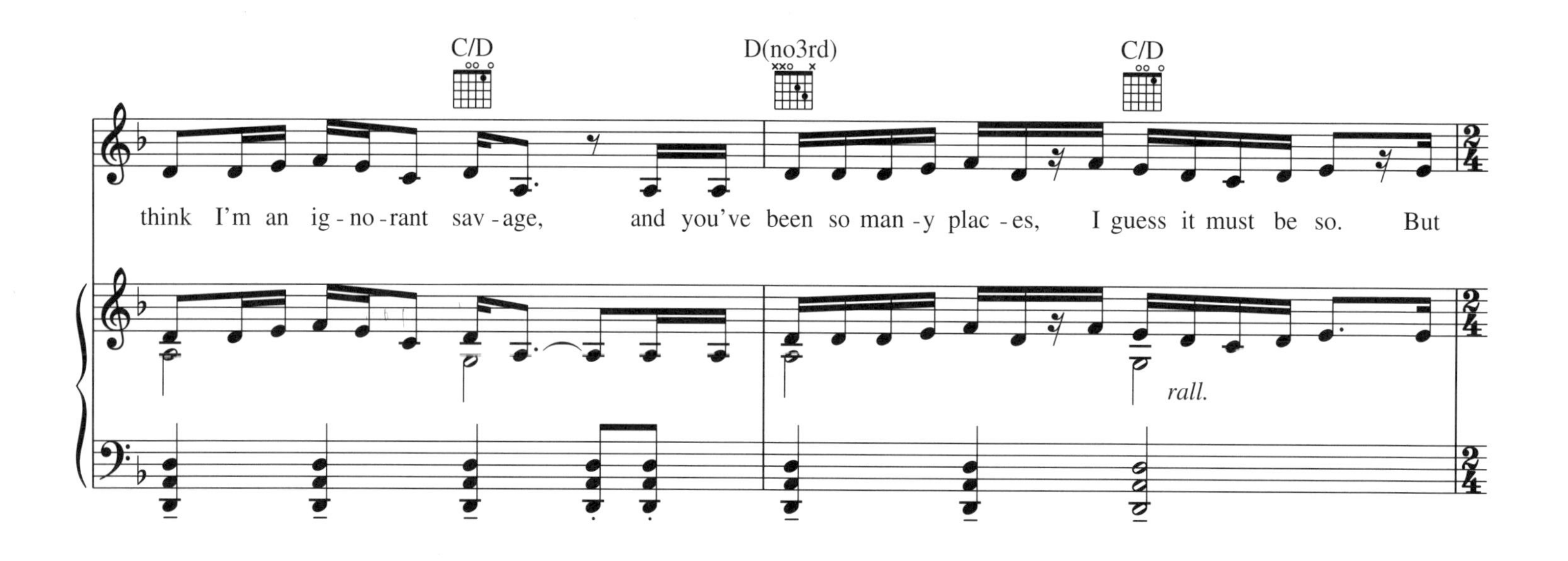

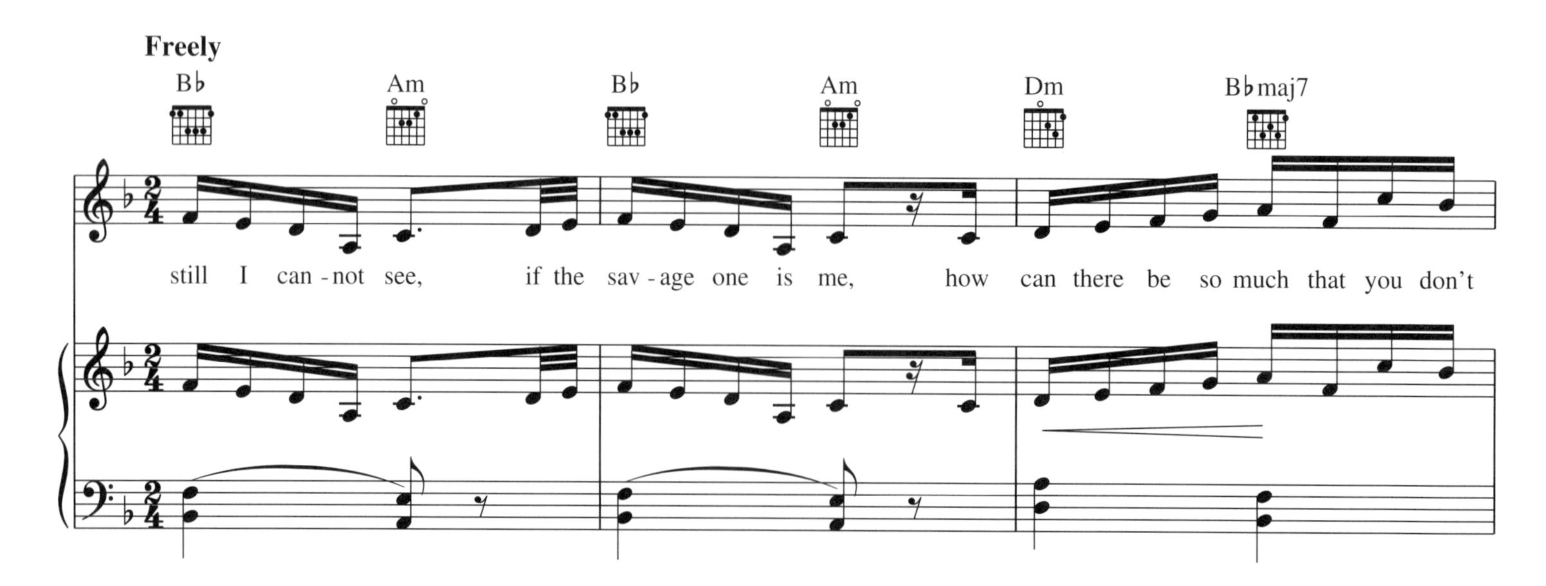

Moderately
A(no3rd)
N.C.
D
Bm
know? You don't know...
mf
D
Bm
You
poco rall.
mp
D
Bm
D
think you own what - ev - er land you land on; the earth is just a dead thing you can
a tempo
F♯m
Bm
G
claim; but I know ev - 'ry rock and tree and crea - ture has a

Em7sus
A9sus
Bm
D
life, has a spir - it, has a name.
You think the on - ly peo - ple who are
Bm
D
F♯m
peo - ple are the peo - ple who look and think like you, but
Bm
G
Em7(add4)
A9sus
if you walk the foot - steps of a strang - er you'll learn things you nev - er knew you nev - er
D
Bm
F♯m
G(add9)
G
knew. Have you ev - er heard the wolf cry to the blue corn moon, or
f *expressively*

Bm
F♯m
G(add9)
A
asked the grin - ning bob - cat why he grinned? Can you sing with all the voic - es of the
D(add9)/F♯
Bm7
2 fr
G6/9
Bm7(add4)
moun - tain? Can you paint with all the col - ors of the wind? Can you
mf
Em7(add4)
A9sus
D
Bm
paint with all the col - ors of the wind?
rit.
ff a tempo
A bit brighter
D
Bm
D
Come run the hid - den pine trails of the
mf
mp poco accel.

Bm
D
F♯m
for - est, come taste the sun-sweet ber-ries of the earth; come
sim.
Bm
Bm/A
G
Em7
A9sus
roll in all the rich-es all a-round you, and for once nev-er won-der what they're
cresc.
Bm
A
D
Bm
worth. The rain-storm and the riv-er are my broth - ers; the
mf
D
F♯m
Bm
her-on and the ot-ter are my friends; and we are all con-nect-ed to each
f poco a poco cresc.

G
Em7
A9sus
D
oth - er in a cir - cle, in a hoop that nev - er ends.
ff
F♯m
G
D(add9)/F♯
Bm
C
How high does the syc - a - more grow? If you cut it down, _ then you'll
f
G/A
A
G/A
A
G/A
A
Bm
nev - er know. _ And you'll nev - er hear the wolf cry to the
rall.
ff a tempo
F♯m
G(add9)
G
Bm
F♯m
blue corn moon, for wheth - er we are white or cop - per - skinned, we need to

G
A
D(add9)/F♯
Bm
G6/9
sing with all the voic - es of the moun - tain, need to paint with all the col - ors of the
mf
Bm7(add4)
Em
A
wind. You can own the earth and still all you'll
F♯m
G
Bm
Gmaj7
G/A
D
own is earth un - til you can paint with all the col - ors of the wind.
rit. e. cresc.
f > mp
a tempo
Bm
G
Em7/A
D
rall.
expressively
p
pp

DAUGHTER OF GOD

Music by ALAN MENKEN
Lyrics by HOWARD ASHMAN

D
A/E
E7sus
E
e - nough, may - be it's my way of
- ur - day and ev - 'ry day be - tween. My
A
D
A
E/G♯
hold - ing back the wa - ters of fenc - ing in the yard.
eyes are on to - mor - row. My lips are on their guard.
F♯m
C♯m
4fr
D
Lord, it gets so lone - some,
A/E
A
Bm7
A7/C♯
Lord, it gets so hard. If I could

D
F♯m
A6
E/G♯
sing like a daugh-ter of God, like a child of the an - gels,
A7
Dsus
D
Esus
E
like a lov-er of Je - sus, like a sis-ter of prayer.
A
Bm7
A7/C♯
D
If I could sing like a daugh-ter of God,
F♯m
A6
E/G♯
A7
To Coda
like a child of the an - gels, if I could sing,

D
E7sus
E
1
A
I would-n't care.
D/A
A
D/E
E
D/E
I
2
A
D/A
A
D/A
A
D/A
Half the world is fro - zen,

A
E/G♯
F♯m
half the world's on fire.
C♯m
4fr
D
Half the world keeps si - lent and
A/E
E7sus
E7
half the world's a choir. If
A
D
A
E/G♯
I could join their voic - es, all loud and sweet and sad,

F♯m
C♯m
4fr
D
it would - n't seem so lone - some.
A/E
Esus
A
D.S. al Coda
Bm7
A7/C♯
It would - n't feel so bad.
If I could
CODA
D
E7sus
E7
I would - n't care.
A
D/A
A
rit.

GO THE DISTANCE

from Walt Disney Pictures' HERCULES

Music by ALAN MENKEN
Lyrics by DAVID ZIPPEL

D E F♯m A/C♯ Dmaj7 Esus E D E A
great warm wel-come will be wait - ing for me. Where the crowds will cheer when they
D E F♯sus F♯m D C♯ F♯m
see my face, and a voice keeps say - ing this is
Dmaj7 Esus E A/C♯ Bm/D
where I'm meant to be. I will find my way.
mf
A/E E E/D A/C♯ Bm/D
I can go the dis - tance. I'll be there some - day

A/E
E
E/D
A/C♯
Dsus2
F♯m7
if I can be strong. I know ev - 'ry mile will be worth my
Bm7
2 fr
D
E
A
A/G♯
F♯m
F♯m/E
Dmaj7
while. I would go most an - y - where to feel like
Esus
E
A
E/A
D/A
I be - long.
lightly
a tempo
mp
poco rall.
A
E/A
D/A
D
E
A

D
E
A
D
E
F#m
Dmaj7
Esus
E
simply
D
E
A
D
E
F#sus
F#m
R.H.
D
C#
F#m
Dmaj7
Esus
E

Dsus2/F♯
E/G♯
A
E/A
D/A
poco rall.
a tempo
7
A
E/A
D/A
F
G
C
mf
F
G
C
F
E
Am
Fmaj7
f
Gsus
3 fr
G
F/A
G/B
C/F
G7
C/E
Dm/F
I am on my way.

C/G G G/F C/E Dm/F C/G G G/F
I can go the dis - tance. I don't care how far, some-how I'll be strong. I know
C/E F Am7 Dm7 C/E
ev - 'ry mile will be worth my while. I would
F G C G/B Am C/G Fmaj7 Gsus G C G
go most an-y-where to find where I be - long.
3 fr
poco rall.
a tempo
C G F G C5
3 fr
rall.
p

GOD BLESS US EVERYONE

from A CHRISTMAS CAROL

Music by ALAN MENKEN
Lyrics by LYNN AHRENS

G
Bm
C6
G/B
Bm
C6
G/B
Bm
In your heart there's a light as bright as a star in
C
D
G
Bm
C6
G/B
Bm
heav - en. Let it shine through the night, and
C
D7sus
D7
G(add9)
D
D7/C
God bless us, ev - 'ry - one.
'Til each
mf
G/B
C
Em
D6
C6
child is fed, 'til all men are free,

G/B
D7/A
G
C6
'til the world be - comes a fam -
B
D7/A
G
Bm
C6
G/B
Bm
'ly... Star by star up a - bove and
C6
G/B
Bm
C
D
G
Bm
kind - ness by hu - man kind - ness, light this
C6
G/B
Bm
C
G/B
D7sus
D7
world with your love, and God bless us, ev - 'ry -

G(add9)
D
D7/C
one.
'Til
each
G/B
C
Em
D6
C6
child is fed,
'til all
men are free,
G/B
D7/A
G
Am/C
'til the
world be - comes a
fam -
B
D/E
E
A
C♯m
D6
A/C♯
C♯m
4 fr
'ly...
Let the
stars in the sky re -
rall.
f a tempo

D6
A/C♯
C♯m
4 fr
D
E
A
mind us of man's com - pas - sion. Let us
Dmaj7/E
love 'til we die, and God bless us, ev -
E7
'ry - one.
poco dim.
C♯m7
Bm/E
God bless _ us, ev - 'ry - one.
8vb

I CAN'T TAKE MY EYES FROM YOU

Music and Lyrics by
ALAN MENKEN

Cm6
G(add9)/B
G/B
C(add2)
might, I'm drawn to you all the same; a
sign. I smile at you, then I blush; a
G/D
B7/D♯
Em(add2)
Em/D
C(add2)
C
help - less moth in - to a flame. As long as you're in
school - boy with a fool - ish crush. But what else can I
G/B
Am7
Bm7
C/D
view,
do?
I can't take my eyes from
1
G
G(add2)/B
C(add2)
G/D
D7sus
D7
you.

2
G
Am7/G
5fr
G
D
Asus2/C♯
A/C♯
you.
An - y - one can tell,
C(add2)
C
Gsus2/B
G/B
D
Am6
an - y - one can see.
An - y - time you're near me I am sud -
B7sus
2fr
B7
Em
Em/D
C(add2)
F♯m7♭5/C
3fr
Gsus2/B
G/B
- den - ly a - glow.
You've got me in your spell, that's
E♭
F/E♭
Dm7
B♭/D
Cm
where I want to be.
Now I see you ev -

E♭maj7/B♭
D7sus
D7
E7sus
E7
A
3fr
-'ry - where I go.
I can't take my
A/C♯
D
A/E
D/F♯
E/G♯
eyes from you, though I've mem - or - ized your face.
You are
A
Amaj7
F♯m9
F♯m/E
B7/D♯
2fr
beau - ti - ful in ev - 'ry light,
ev - 'ry style and
Dm6
Asus2/C♯
A/C♯
D
A/E
C♯/E
ev - 'ry place.
Tell me it's all in my mind,
tell me that my

F♯m
F♯/E
D(add2)
Asus2/C♯
F♯m7
love is blind. I know that could be true, but
Bm7
Asus2/C♯
A/C♯
D/E
A
Asus2/C♯
D
I can't take my eyes from you.
A/E
D/F♯
E/G♯
A
D
I can't take my eyes from you.
rit.
Slowly
A/E
D/E
E/G♯
A
I can't take my eyes from you.

I WANNA BE A ROCKETTE

Music by ALAN MENKEN
Lyrics by TOM EYEN

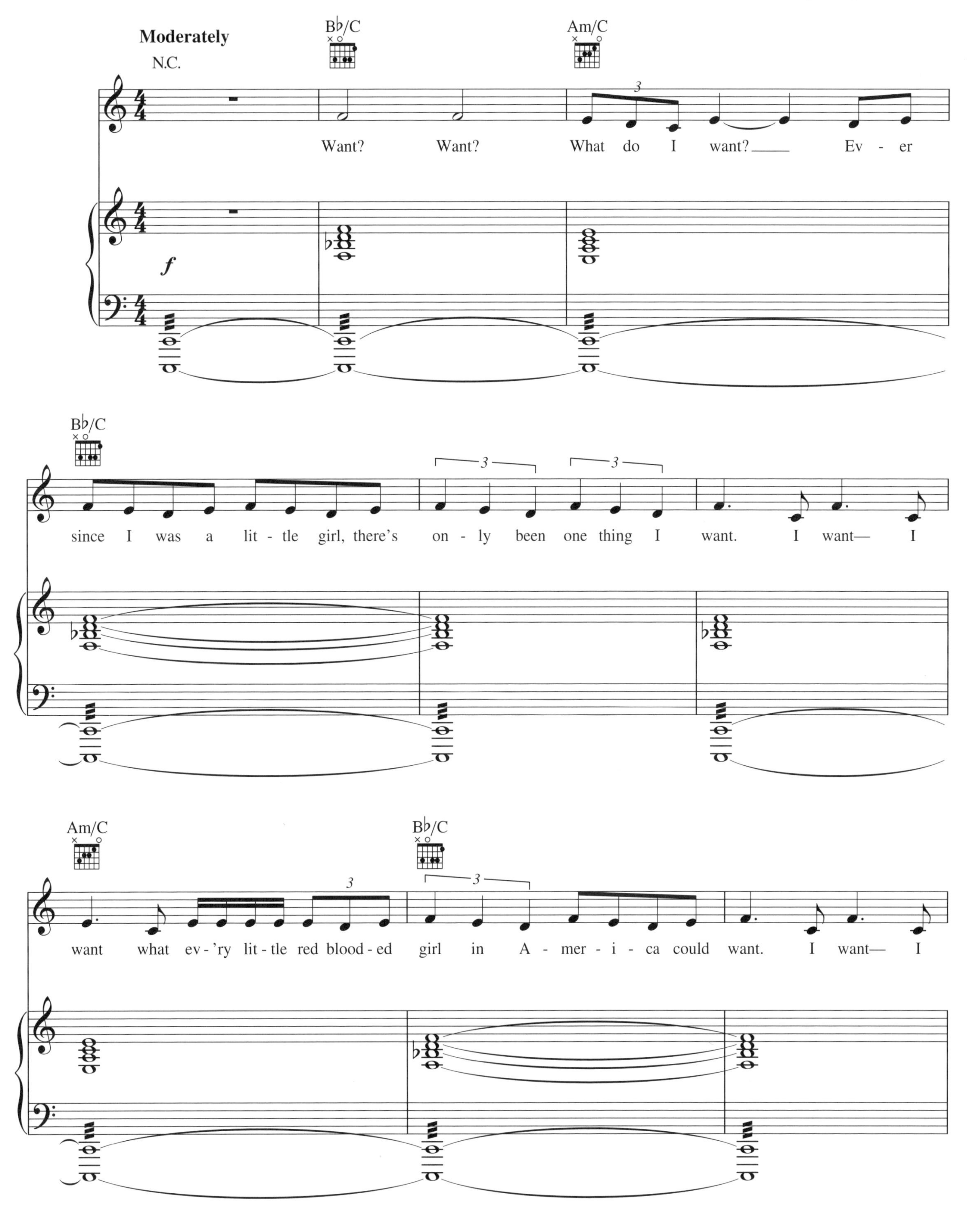

B♭maj7/C
Am7/C
B♭/C
want what I have want - ed since the first day I learned how to want:
A tempo - Bright 4
N.C.
Fmaj9
I want to be a Rock - ette.
I want to dance un - til dawn.
ff
mp
Gm9
3fr
Am7
I want to be a Rock - ette,
that's what my heart
Dm7
Gm7
Am7
Bmaj7/C
3fr
C7
is set up - on.
I want to be a Rock - ette.
ff

G(add2)/A
A7
G(add2)/A
A7
Dm
I want to hear the crowd roar.
Dm/C
Bm7♭5
G7
F/A
I want to feel the mag - ic when they scream for more and more and
B♭m6
6fr
G7/B
C7sus
Am/C
more and more and... I nev - er want - ed to be some - bod - y's wife;
sub. p
C7sus
Am/C
Gm7
Fmaj7/A
a sub - ur - ban life seems a pit - y.

B♭ C7sus C/D D6
I nev - er want - ed to be a mov - ie star.
sub. p
C/D D6 Gm7
I al - ways want - ed to be a danc - er at Ra - di - o
B♭maj7/C Am7/C B♭maj7/C Am7/C B♭maj7/C Am7/C B♭maj7/C Am7/C B♭maj7/C
Cit - y.
Fmaj9
I want to be a Rock - ette and it's no sur - prise.

Gm9
3fr
B♭maj7/C
Am7
I want to be a Rock-ette,
oh how my foot
Dm7
Gm7
Am7
B♭maj7/C
C7
2fr
is gon - na rise.
I want to be a Rock - ette;
G(add2)/A
A7
G(add2)/A
A7
Dm
it's one thing I know.
And when I'm
Dm/C
Bm7♭5
G7
F/A
a Rock-ette, I'll nev - er miss one show.
I'll show em! I'll show

B♭m
Bdim
B♭/C
Am/C
em! I'll show em!
I nev-er want-ed to be a Broad-way star;
B♭/C
Am/C
Gm7
F/A
B♭
Fsus/C
be-ing fa-mous has too man-y du-ties.
D♭sus2/E♭
4fr
Cm/E♭
3fr
D♭sus2/E♭
4fr
I nev-er want-ed to be a bal-let star;
I al-ways
Cm/E♭
3fr
Gm7
B♭/C
Am/C
want-ed to be
one of those daz-zl-ing danc-ing beau-

B♭/C
Am/C
B♭/C
Am/C
B♭/C
N.C.
- ties.
I'll al - ways re - mem -
C7/G
F
- ber when Ma - ma brought me to New York and I first saw those
C/E
Dm
F/C
Bm7♭5
E7/G♯
girls up on the stage; there was mag - ic ev - 'ry -
Am
E/G♯
Gm7
Am/G
Gm
Am/G
where. "Look at them, Ma - ma", I said.

Gm7
Am/G
Gm7
Am/G
B♭/C
"One of these days your lit - tle girl's gon - na be up there.
Am/C
C/D
Bm/D
C/D
Bm/D
C/D
Bm/D
I'm gon - na be up there."
poco a poco rall.
C/D
Bm/D
C/D
Bm/D
C/D
Gmaj7
I'm gon - na be a Rock - ette;
f slightly slower
Gmaj9
Am7
D7
Am9
5fr
Cmaj7/D
5fr
let me out on that stage.
I'm gon - na be a Rock - ette,
accel. poco a poco
3
simile

A tempo
Bm7
Em7
Am7
Bm7
they are the great - est danc - ers of our
Cmaj7/D
5fr
D7
A/B
B7/F♯
A/B
B7/F♯
age. I'm gon - na be a Rock - ette; I'm gon - na hear the crowd scream.
Em
Em/D
C♯m7♭5
4fr
I'm gon - na know the feel - ing of get - ing my
A7
G/D
E♭+
dream. And that is my dream, to know how it feels, to be some - one who's free

Em
A7sus
A7
Am7
and kicks up her heels. It's what I was meant to be.
Double-time feel
Gsus2/B
C/D
Bm/D
You got - ta take me. Got - ta take me. Got - ta take
C/D
D7
G
Em
me— got - ta take me! Got - ta take me!
G
Em
G(add2)
Me!
ff

IF I CAN'T LOVE HER

from Walt Disney's BEAUTY AND THE BEAST: THE BROADWAY MUSICAL

Music by ALAN MENKEN
Lyrics by TIM RICE

C♭
Cm
3fr
no com - fort, no es - cape.
I see, but deep with - in is
With more motion
Fm
Gsus
G7
Em
B♭
C/B♭
ut - ter blind - ness.
Hope - less,
as my
rall.
F/A
C/G
F6/9
C/E
dream dies.
As the time flies,
love a
Dm/F
Em/G
F/A
G/B
Em
B♭
C/B♭
lost il - lu - sion.
Help - less,
un - for -
a tempo

F/A
C/G
F6/9
C/E
giv - en.
Cold and driv - en
to this
Moderately
Dm/F
Em/G
F/A
G/B
C
Dm7(add4)
sad con - clu - sion.
No beau - ty could
rit.
dim.
mp tenderly
C/E
Fmaj7
F6
C/G
F/A
G/B
C
G/B
move me, no good - ness im - prove me.
Am
Dm7
C/E
F
Fmaj7/G
Fmaj7/A
No pow - er on Earth, if I can't love

78

E♭m
G♭7/D♭
3rd time To Coda
A♭7/C
A♭m7♭5
bout! And thus it did - n't mat - ter when they
hell... Though the guys were dou - bled o - ver, and the
works. I
G♭(add2)/B♭
E♭m9
A♭m7(add13)
D♭13
chuck - led at my hue. I was ten, I was blue and I
prin - ci - pal: hoo hoo! He's of - fend - ed, I'm sus - pend - ed, but I
1
G♭maj7
G♭m7
G♭maj7
D♭7sus
knew.
G♭maj7
G♭m7
G♭maj7
D♭7sus
In

G/B F/A G7/B C Dm7(add4) C/E Fmaj7 F6
her. No pas - sion could reach me,
C/G F/A G/B C G/B Am Dm7
no les - son could teach me how I could have
poco cresc.
C/E F Am Em B♭
loved her and make her love me too. If I
dim.
Agitated
F/A Fm/A♭ G7 Am
can't love her, then who?
rit.
mf

Am
Dm/A
G
Em
Am
Long a - go, I should have seen
sim.
Am
Dm/A
G
Em
Am
all the things I could have been.
sfz
sim.
B♭
F/A
B♭
C/B♭
Gm7
3fr
Care - less and un - think - ing, I moved
sfz
sim.
Asus
A
on - ward!
f
rall.

F♯m C D/C G/B

ff a tempo

D/A G6/9 D/F♯

Em/G F♯m/A G/B A/C♯ D Em7sus

rall.

f a tempo

No pain could be deep - er. No life could be cheap - er.

D/F♯ Gmaj7 G6 D/A G/B A/C♯ D A/C♯

Bm
Em7
D/F♯
G
Gmaj7/A
Gmaj7/B
No point an - y - more, if I can't love
A/C♯
G/B
A/C♯
F
Gm7sus
her. No spir - it could
8va
ff
F/A
B♭
F/C
B♭/D
win me. No hope left with -
loco
C/E
F
C/E
Dm
Gm7
3fr
F/A
B♭
in me, hope I could have loved her and that she'd

Dm
Am
E♭
3fr
B♭/D
set me free. But it's not to
mf moving ahead
B♭m6/D♭
3fr
F/C
C7sus
C7
B♭/C
C
be. If I can't love her,
Gm/C
3fr
Am/C
B♭/C
Am/C
B♭/C
F
D♭
let the world be done with me.
rall. e cresc.
ff
a tempo
broadening
F

IF I NEVER KNEW YOU
(Love Theme from POCAHONTAS)
from Walt Disney's POCAHONTAS

Music by ALAN MENKEN
Lyrics by STEPHEN SCHWARTZ

G
Em
C
if I nev - er felt this love, I would have no ink -
Am7
C
D7sus
- ling of how pre - cious life can be.
G
Em
G
And if I nev - er held you, I would nev - er have
Em7
E7/G♯
Am(add9)
5fr
Cm(maj7)
3fr
Cm6
a clue how, at last, I'd find in you

Em9
Bm/D
C
Am6(add2)
Cmaj7/D
D9
the miss-ing part of me.
In this world so full of fear,
Am6(add2)
Cmaj7/D
D9
Bm7
B7/D♯
Em11
Em7
full of rage and lies,
I can see the truth so clear
C
D
C/D
G
Em
in your eyes, so dry your eyes.
And I'm so grate - ful to you.
G
G/B
C
Am7
G/B
I'd have lived my whole life through,
lost for - ev - er

C
C/D
C
Am
if I nev - er knew you.
There's no mo - ment
C
Am
F
I re - gret
since the mo - ment
that we met.
C/D
Dm
F
F/G
G
F/G
If our time has
gone too fast
I've lived at last.
G♭/A♭
D♭
B♭m
And
if I nev - er
knew you,

D♭
Fm7
G♭maj7
E♭m7
Fm7
I'd have lived my whole life through emp - ty as the sky,
G♭(add9)
E♭m7
Fm7
G♭maj7
nev - er know - ing why,
rit.
Freely
B♭m7
D♭/F
G♭
A♭7sus
A♭7
4fr
D♭
lost for - ev - er if I nev - er knew you.
a tempo
B♭m
G♭
A♭7
D♭(add9)
rit.

NEED TO KNOW

Music by ALAN MENKEN
Lyrics by DAVID SPENCER

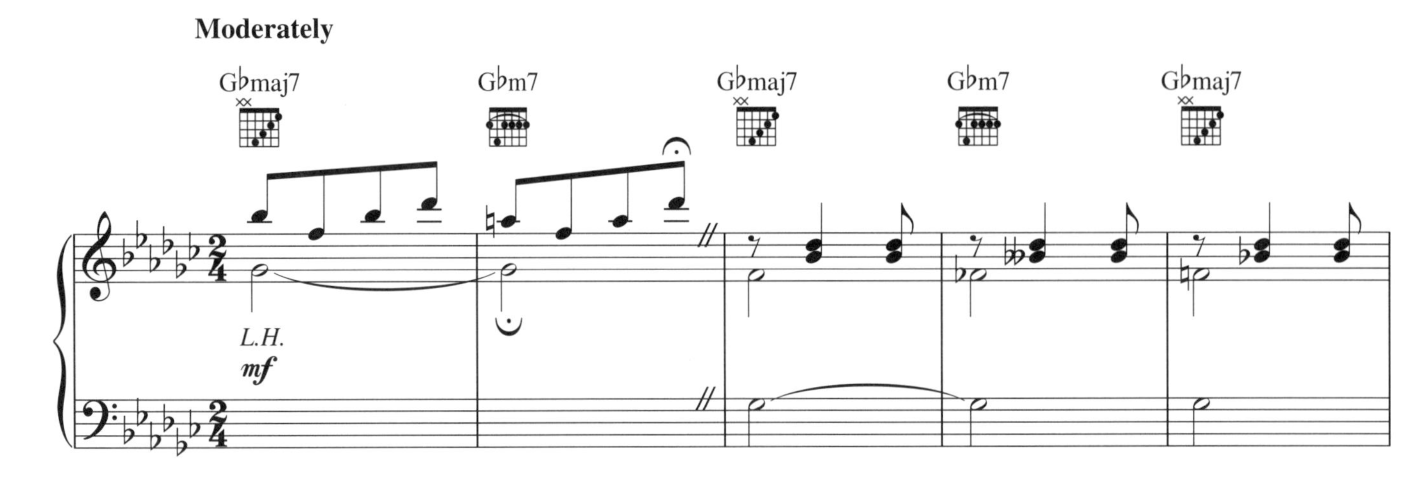

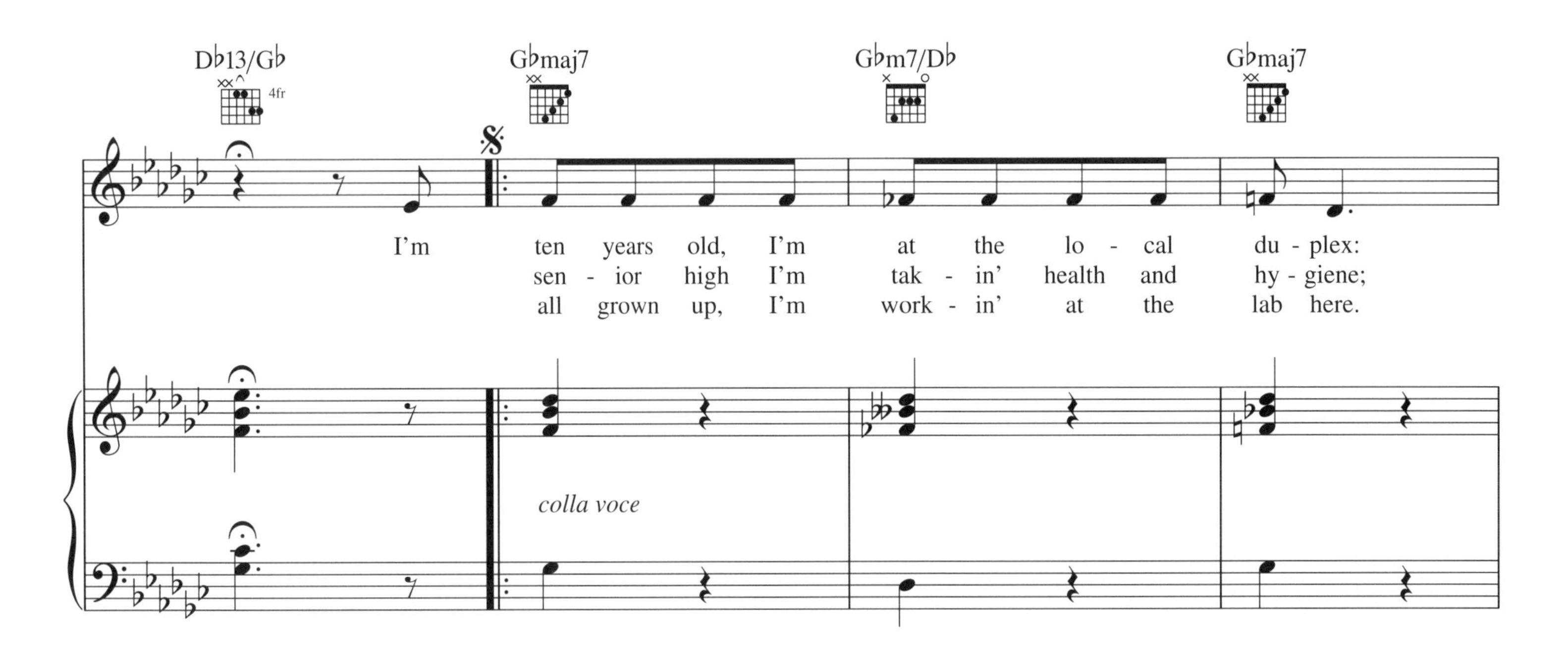

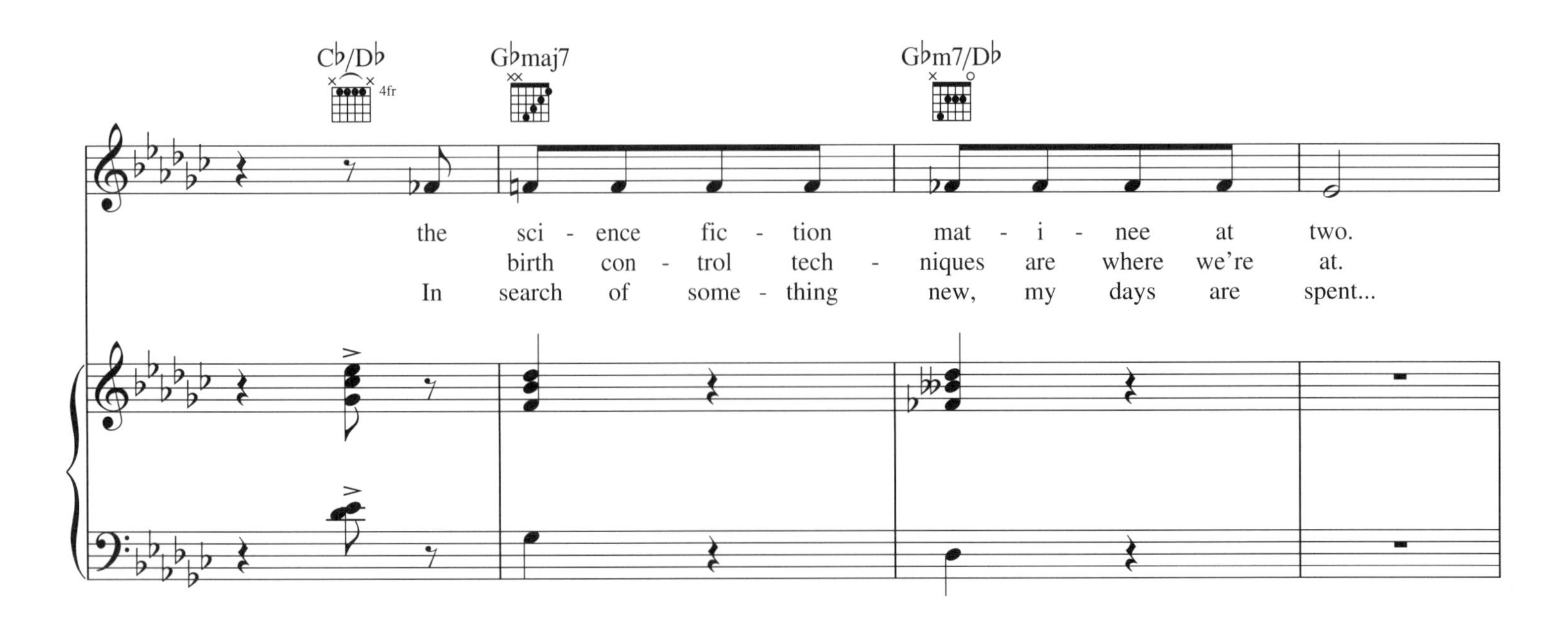

75

E♭7
Cm7♭5
F7
B♭m7
I don't re - call the mov - ie but the a - li - ens were
The teach - er's go - in' on how best and strong - est is the
When this ho - lo - graph - ic deal starts be - hav - in' like she's
E♭7
G♭/A♭
A♭9
D♭7sus
groov - y and I won - dered, how'd they make the ac - tors blue?
con - dom, and I'm won - der - in': well, just how strong is that?
real! Sil - ly me. I'm think - in' this is an e - vent!
D♭7
G♭maj7
G♭m7/D♭
G♭maj7
C♭/D♭
So— when I get home I fill the tub with fizz - ies
So— comes the year - ly sci - ence com - pe - ti - tion...
Doc— It frames the su - per - na - tur - al in sci - ence.
N.C.
G♭maj7
G♭m7/D♭
E♭7sus
thir - ty for - ty fizz - ies, pur - ple grape.
I snap the sheet, my pro - ject is un - veiled;
It chang - es me - ta - phys - ics in - to fact.

E♭7
Cm7♭5
F7
B♭m7
I soak for sev - en ho - urs. I get these fun - ny
"The Rub - ber Pro - phy - lac - tic: How It Func - tions Un - der
Is there some - thing af - ter dy - ing, like an af - ter - life or
E♭7
G♭/A♭
A♭7
4fr
C♭/D♭
4fr
A♭m7
4fr
streaks. They won't come off in show - ers, peo - ple laugh at me for
Stress..." The fac - es on the fa - cul - ty, you'd think I wore a
God? And a rea - son why you're sigh - ing like you find my in - t'rest
D♭7
4fr
D♭
G♭maj7
E♭m9
4fr
weeks. But I knew, thought I
dress. But I knew, had it
odd? I don't know, but I
8va
loco
A♭m7
4fr
D♭9
B♭m7
E♭9
knew. And at ten that was a might - y head - y
graphed for the rub - ber tip, the re - ser - voir, the
will. You can bet your chips and di - odes that I

A♭m7 D♭9 A A/G♯
brew. On my skin... in my
shaft; had ma - chines test - ing
will. If it's war, then it's
F♯m7 A/E A♭7sus A♭7
hair... And I fell in love with re - search then and
length; li - quid mer - cu - ry for gaug - ing ten - sile
war. Con - se - quenc - es nev - er
D♭9sus D♭7 G♭maj7 E♭m9
there... And I thought, "Check it
strength. How'd I do? Hard to
both - ered me be - fore. Ain't the fame. Ain't the
A♭m7 D♭9 B♭7sus B♭7/D
out!" I've locked in - to what my life is all a -
tell. See, the girls thought it was int - 'rest - ing as
perks. It's the sim - ple find - ing out how some - thing

2
N.C.
knew.
And I
dim.
D E/D Asus2/C♯ A/C♯ D E/D Asus2/C♯ A/C♯
need to know. The un - known steps up to dare me. Then I
Bm7 C♯7 F♯m Amaj7/E D♯m7♭5 G♯7
tell it, "You don't scare me," with my head be - tween its
C♯sus2 C♯ Bm7 E9 Asus2 A
jaws. "Why" – now that's a beau - ti - ful word, the

Bm7
E9
Asus2
A
F♯m9
G♯7sus
G♯7
sec - ond best there is. The ver - y best there is is "Be -
Tempo I
C♯7sus
C♯7
C♯m7
C♯7
D.S. al Coda
cause." I'm
CODA
A♭/C
Bdim7
B♭m7
fig - ure, here's a mys - ter - y just wait - ing to be
pp
cresc.
E♭m7
A♭/C
Bdim7
B♭m7
solved. And yes, I'm get - ting pissed cuz you don't wan - na get in -

Ebm7
Ab/C
Bdim7
Bbm7
volved. Go read the job de - scrip - tion, Doc, dis - cov - er - ing this
Ebm7
Ab7
Gb(add2)/Bb
shit is what we do. I
Abm7b5/Cb
Ab7/C
Cbm
Abm7/Cb
want to feel like I'm ten all
Gb
Bbm7
Gb
Gbmaj7
o - ver a - gain, that

E♭m
D♭6/9
C♭
G♭/B♭
swell time when I was
D♭7sus
D♭
D♭m7/A♭
D♭7
blue and I
G♭maj7
G♭m7
G♭maj7
D♭7sus
D♭7sus2
knew...
Dm
G♭
(Spoken:) Why not you?

KING OF NEW YORK

from Walt Disney's NEWSIES

Lryics by JACK FELDMAN
Music by ALAN MENKEN

F#/A#
B
C#m
B/D#
C#m/E
C#m/E#
F#/A#
B
G#m9
(2nd time only)
Denton: How 'bout that! I'm
Racetrack: Look at me. I'm the king of New York.
Newsies: Tip your hat. He's the king of New York.
A#m7
B
C#
F#
B
C#m
B/D#
E
A
the king of New York.
Sud - den - ly I'm re - spec - ta - ble. Star -
Newsies: In noth - ing flat he'll be cov - er - ing Brook -
E/A
D
E/D
C#7sus/D
C#7
F#sus
F#
- in' right at 'cha lous - y with sta - ture. Jack: Nob - bin' with all the muck -
- lyn to Tren - ton, our man Den - ton. Kid Blink: Mak - in' a head - line out
D#m
B
G#m
F#/C#
C#
- et - y mucks. I'm blow - in' my dough and go - in' de - luxe. Racetrack: And
Denton: of a hunch, Racetrack: pro - tect - in' the weak and pay - in' for lunch. Denton: When

F♯ B C♯m B/D♯ E A E/A D
4fr 4fr
Racetrack & Jack:
there I be. Ain't I pret - ty? It's my cit - y. I'm
Racetrack: Racetrack & Denton:
I'm at bat strong men crum - ble. Proud yet hum - ble I'm he's
E7/D C♯7sus/D C♯7
1
F♯m
the king of New York!
the king of New
All: I
R.H.
2
F♯m
Boots: A York.
got - ta be ei - ther
dead or dream - in' 'cause look at that pape with my face beam - in'. To -

Gm
3fr
mor - row they may wrap fish - es in it, but I was a star for
one whole min - ute.
G/B
C
F/A
B♭
E/G♯
A
D/F♯
G
C/E
F
B♭/D
D7
G/B
C
Dm
Start - in' now I'm

C/E Dm/F D7/F♯ G C Am9 Bm7 C D
5fr
Denton: Ain't ya heard I'm the king of New
the king of New York.
G C Dm C/E F B♭ F/B♭ E♭
3fr
York.
All: Ho - ly cow, it's a mir - a - cle. Pul - it - zer's cry - in'; Wea -
F/E♭ Cm/E♭ D7 Gsus G Em
3fr 3fr
- sel, he's dy - in'. Flash - pots are shoot - in' bright as the sun, I'm
C Am G/D D G C Dm
one high fa - lu - tin' son of a gun, Don't ask me how for -

C/E F B♭ F/B♭ E♭ 3fr F7/E♭ E♭6 D7
- tune found me. Fate just crowned me. Now I'm king of New
G C Dm C/E F B♭ F/B♭ E♭ 3fr
York.
Look and see once a pik - er, now a strik - er. I'm
F7/E♭ E♭6 D7 G C Dm C/E F B♭
the king of New York.
Vic - to - ry! Front page sto - ry, guts
F/B♭ E♭ 3fr F7/E♭ E♭6 D7 G
and glo - ry. I'm the king of New York!

NEVER AGAIN

Music by ALAN MENKEN
Lyrics by TIM RICE

C
F
Am
No - ble in - ten - tions, words oh so
Dsus
D
F
C/E
fine. Nev - er a - gain will you let me down,
Am7
D7sus
D7
F
nev - er a - gain will I pine.
Nev - er a -
G7sus
G7
C
G7/C
C
G7sus
G
gain will you call your - self mine.

C
G7/C
C/E
F
Why did you change so? No real ex - pla -
mp
Am
G/B
C
Cmaj7/E
na - tion. Still un - a - ware of
F
Am
G/B
C
my hu - mi - li - a - tion. Calm - ly ex -
F
Am
Dsus
D
pect - ing life to go on.

F
C/E
Am7
Nev - er a - gain will I be a - shamed, nev - er a -
D7sus
D
F
G7sus
G7
gain put up - on. Nev - er a - gain will I turn and you're
C
G7/C
C
G7/D
C/E
F
gone. I'd give the world to be - lieve
Gsus
3fr
G
F/C
C
G7/D
C/E
noth - ing has hap - pened.

F
D7/F♯
G7sus
I'd give my heart to the man I once knew.
poco rall.
G7
Dm7
G
E♭
3fr
B7/E♭
Oh, how you loved me!
f slightly broader
E♭maj7/G
A♭
4fr
Cm
3fr
B♭/D
E♭
3fr
Strong, pas - sion - ate, gen - tle. Now you per -
E♭/G
3fr
A♭
4fr
Cm
3fr
B♭/D
ceive me all but in - ci - den - tal.

E♭
3fr
A♭
4fr
Cm
3fr
Words count for noth - ing, on - ly for
Fsus
F
A♭
4fr
E♭/G
3fr
show. Nev - er a - gain will I suf - fer this,
sub. p
Cm7
3fr
F7sus
F7
A♭
4fr
E♭/G
3fr
nev - er a - gain fall so low. Nev - er a -
mf
Fm7
B♭7sus
B♭7
Cm
3fr
Cm7/B♭
6fr
gain but there's one thing I know,
poco rall.

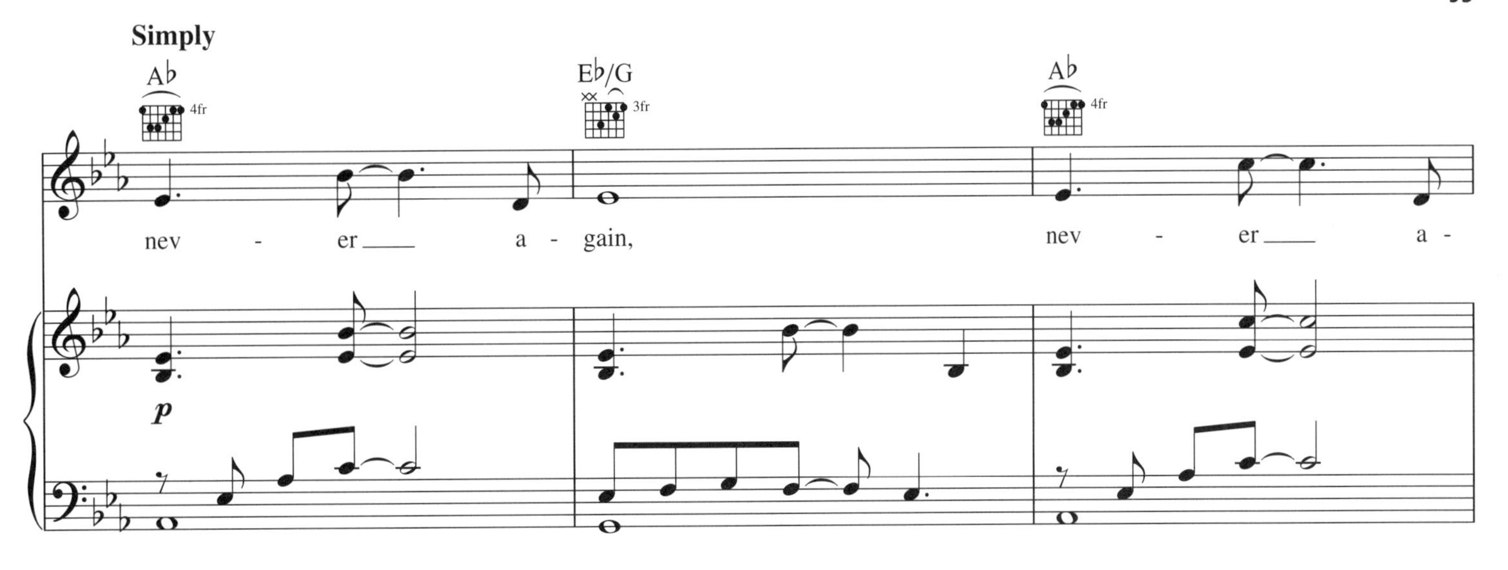
Simply
A♭
4fr
E♭/G
3fr
A♭
4fr
nev - er a - gain,
nev - er a -
p

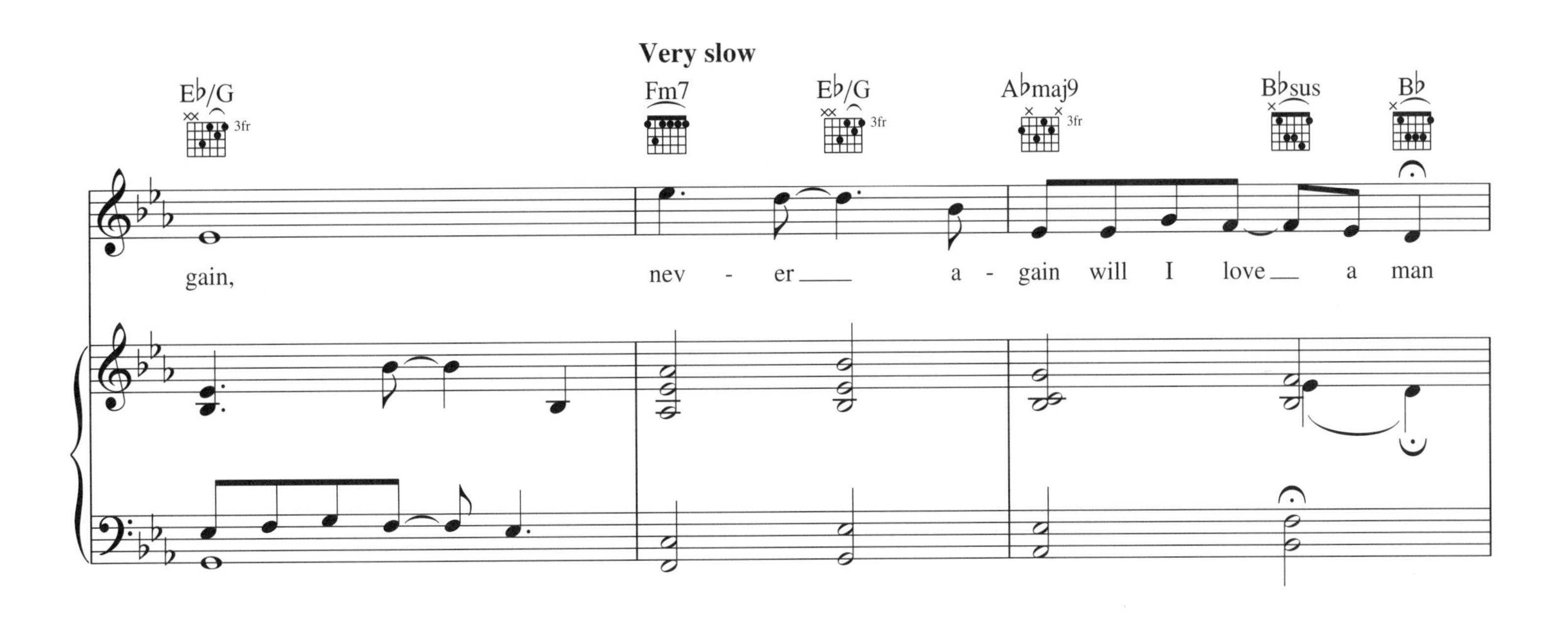
Very slow
E♭/G
3fr
Fm7
E♭/G
3fr
A♭maj9
3fr
B♭sus
B♭
gain,
nev - er a - gain will I love a man

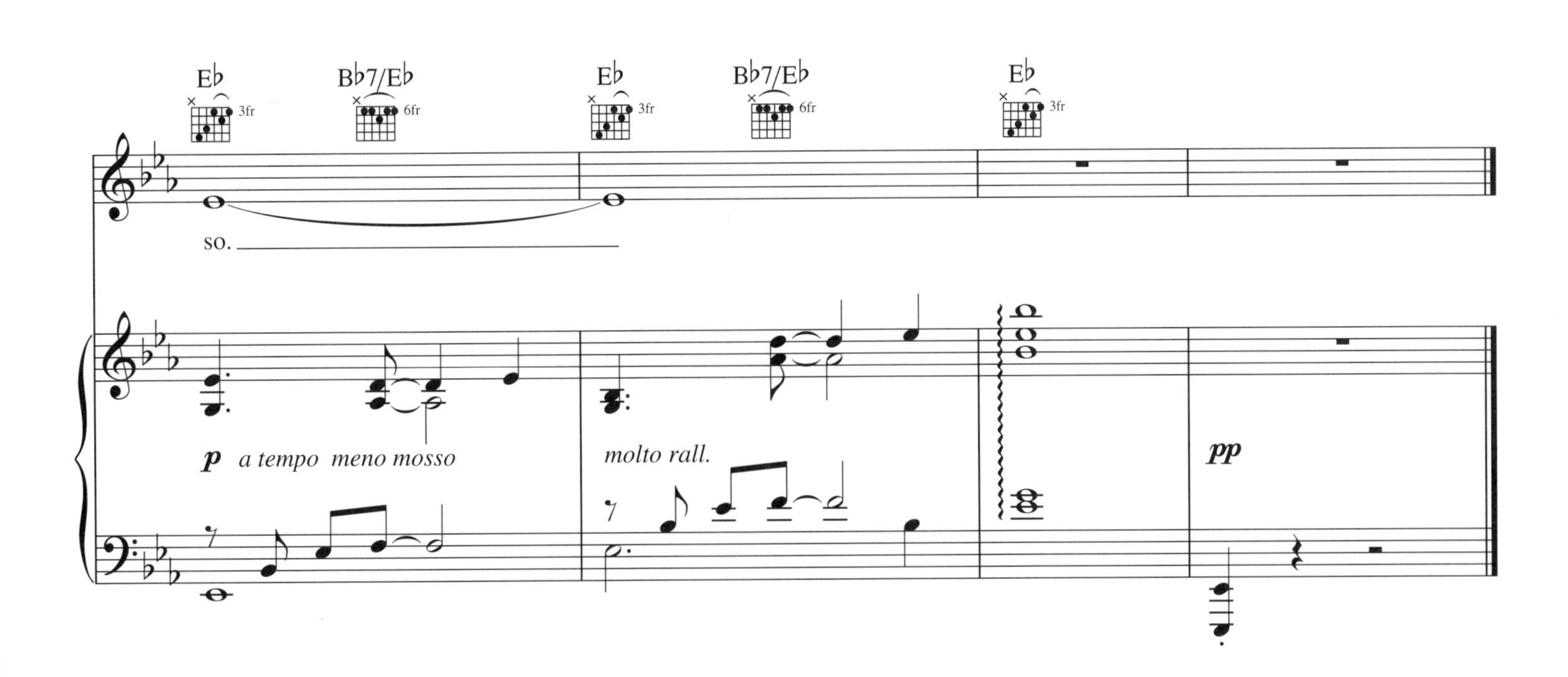
E♭
3fr
B♭7/E♭
6fr
E♭
3fr
B♭7/E♭
6fr
E♭
3fr
so.
p a tempo meno mosso
molto rall.
pp

SHOOTING STAR

Music by ALAN MENKEN
Lyrics by DAVID ZIPPEL

Am Bm/A Am/D D C/G G Bm7/E A7sus A7
And they're right; I'm not sup-posed to be here. I'm com-plete-ly out of
When the sun is set-ting, it's the right time for pre-tend-ing I'm not
Dsus D C Em
place. Some-how there has got to be a rea-son.
here. Some-times I just stare in-to the heav-ens,
B7 C Am7
Eve-nings as I try to think it through, there's a bolt from the
won-d'ring if the an-swer is in sight. That's when I see the
G/B D7 G Em7 D/F♯ G(add2)
blue and I see a shoot-ing star set a-
light of my stead-fast shoot-ing star on his

Em B/D# G7/D Cmaj7 B7
4fr
part from all the rest while the oth - er stars are stand -
way to who knows where. He's so un - like all the stars
Em7 A9 G/F F Cm6/Eb D
5fr
- ing still. He's on a quest. Ev - 'ry
that he out - shines up there. And this
G Em7 D/F# G(add2) Em B/D#
4fr
night this shoot - ing star darts a - cross the twi - light
sol - i - tar - y star is an aw - ful lot like
G7/D C#m7b5 Cm6 1 G/B A7
4fr 3fr
sky, 'cause he knows he does - n't quite fit in and he's
me, on an end - less search through time

F
Cm6/E♭
D
G(add2)
C6/9
long - ing to know why.
G(add2)
C6/9
2
G/B
B♭dim7
and space for a
Slower
Am7
D7sus
D7
Em
A7sus
A7
place that won't seem wrong.
If we
8va
G/D
C♯m7♭5
4fr
Cm(maj7)
8fr
both hang on for long e - nough, if we both some-how are

G/B
D/E
E7
Am11
3fr
strong e - nough,
we'll find out where
Original Tempo
C/D
G(add2)
we be - long.
C6/9
G(add2)
Cmaj7
C6
G(add2)
C(add2)
G(add2)
N.C.

PINK FISH

Music and Lyrics by
ALAN MENKEN

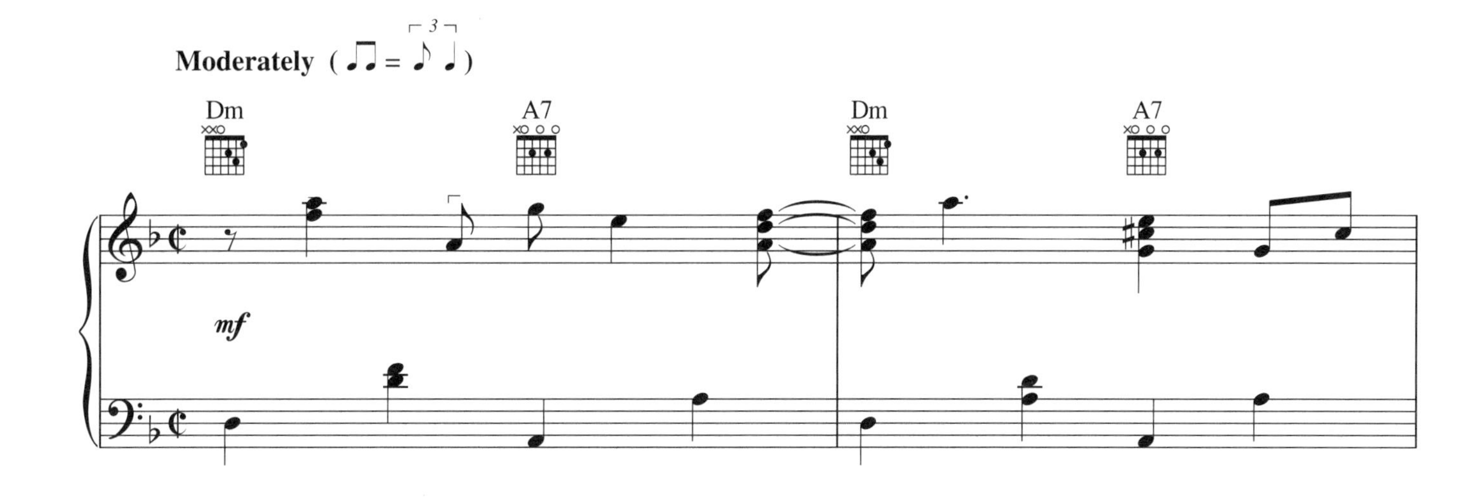

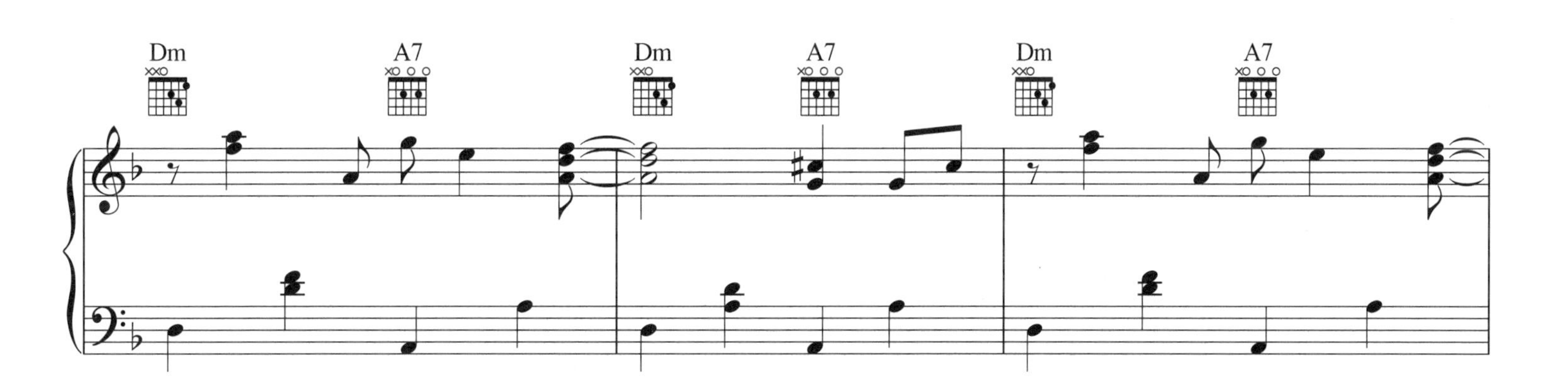

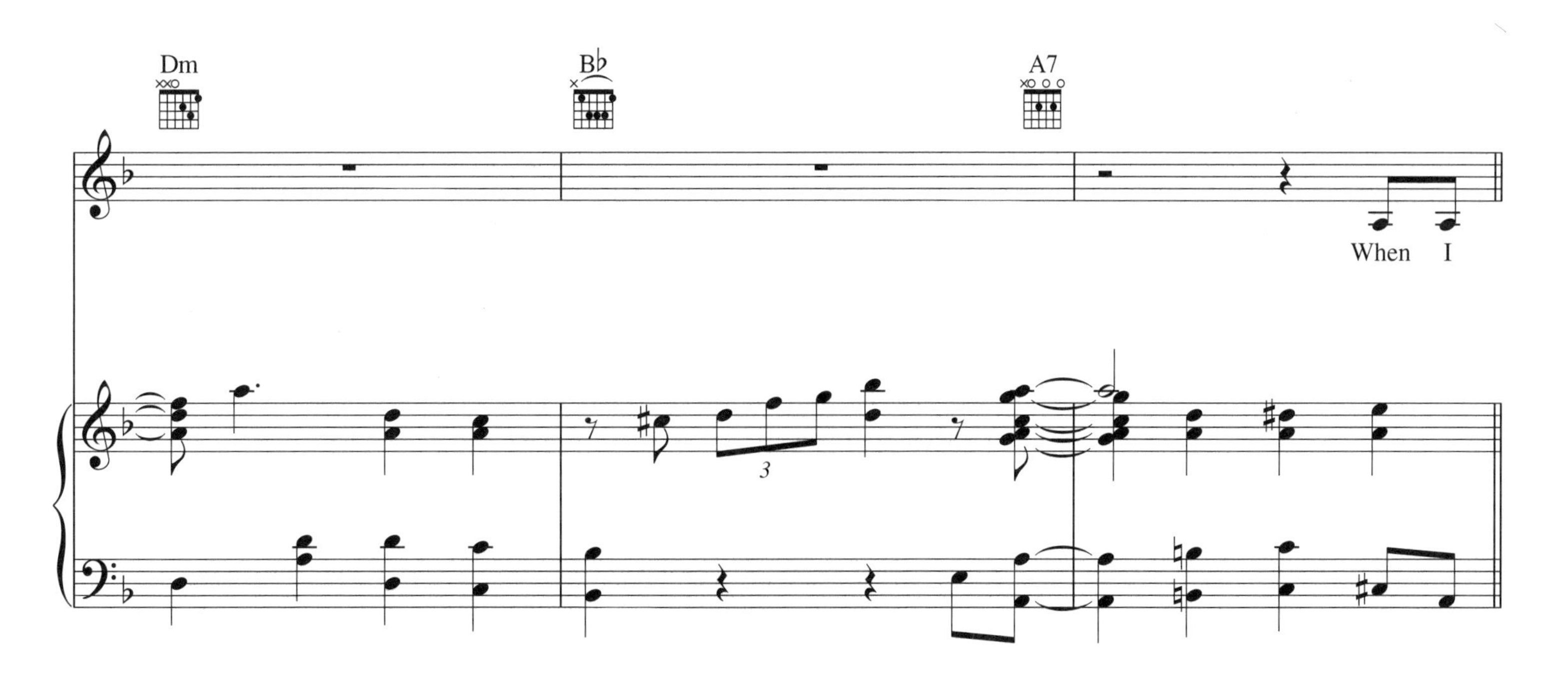

Dm
A7
Dm
A7
first saw New York Cit - y I felt a
went to my first au - di - tion for

Dm
A7
Dm
A7
weak - ness in my knees. So I
Fid - dl - er On The Roof. When I

Dm
A7
Dm
Am/C
went to a ko - sher del - i and
saw the oth - er ac - tors there, I

B♭7
A7♯5
Dm
Em7
Ddim/F
D/F♯
Gm7
C7
2fr
asked for a ham and cheese. No cheese? No
thought I made a goof. No bean - ie, no
F(add2)
F/C
Fsus/G
C7
2fr
ham? I guess I don't know where I am.
beard. Guess I must - 've looked kind - a weird.
F(add2)
F
Fsus/G
C7
2fr
F(add2)
F/D
A - mer - i - can as ap - ple pie,
But when I heard it was a re - li - gious show,

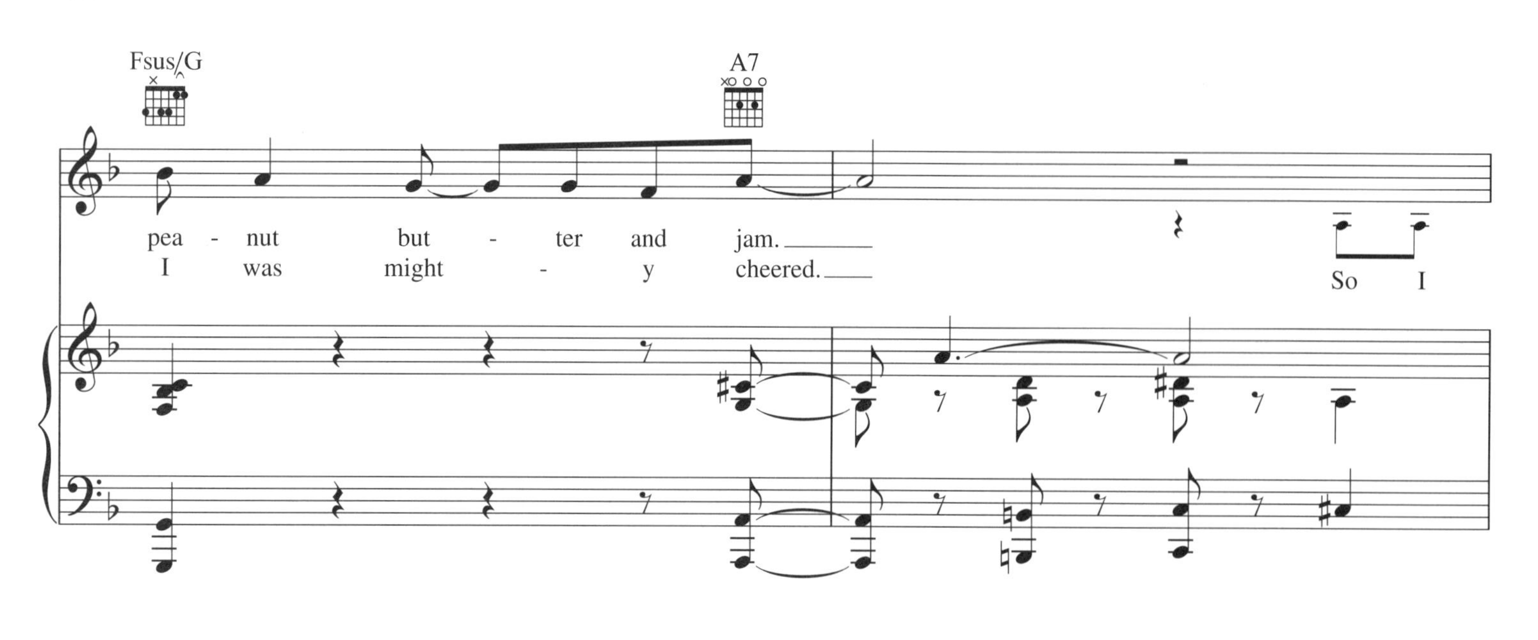
Fsus/G
A7
pea - nut but - ter and jam.
I was might - y cheered.
So I

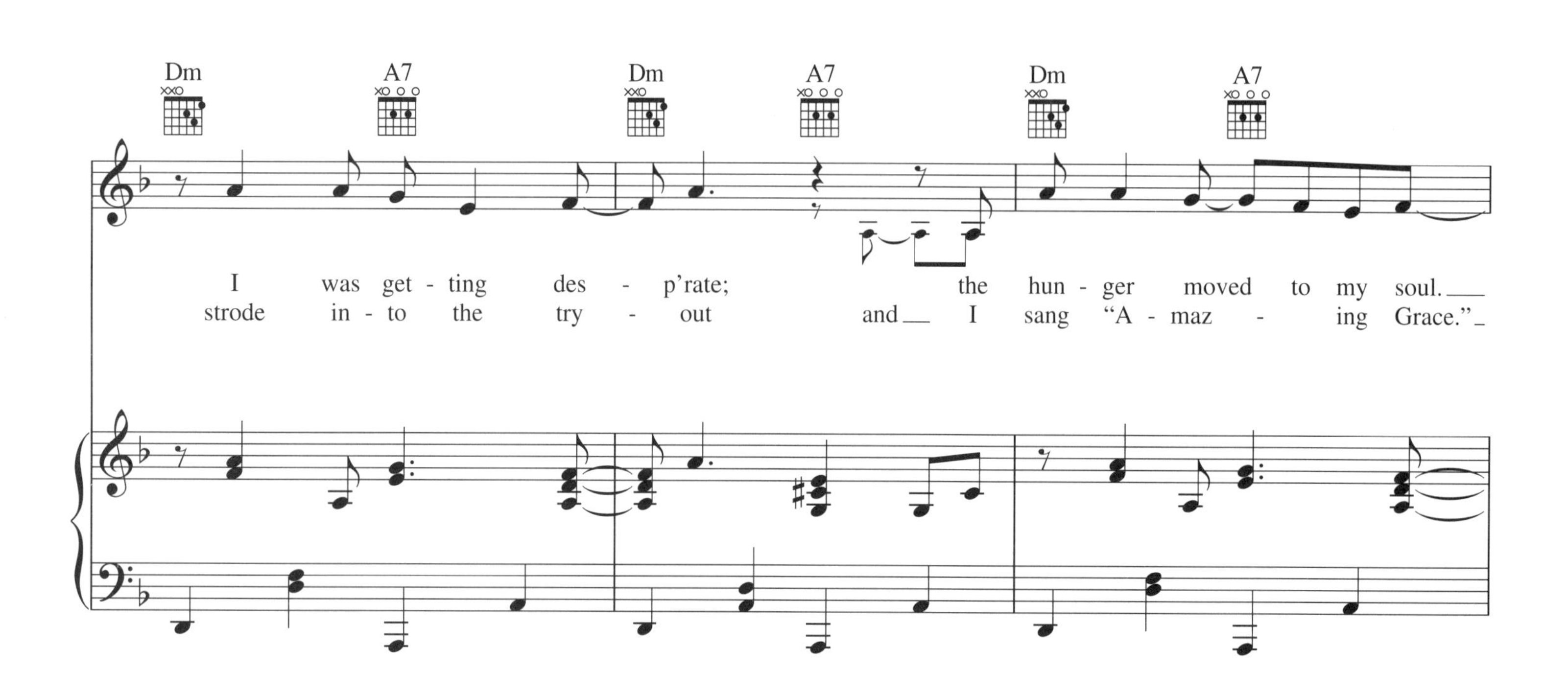
Dm
A7
Dm
A7
Dm
A7
I was get - ting des - p'rate; the hun - ger moved to my soul.
strode in - to the try - out and I sang "A - maz - ing Grace."

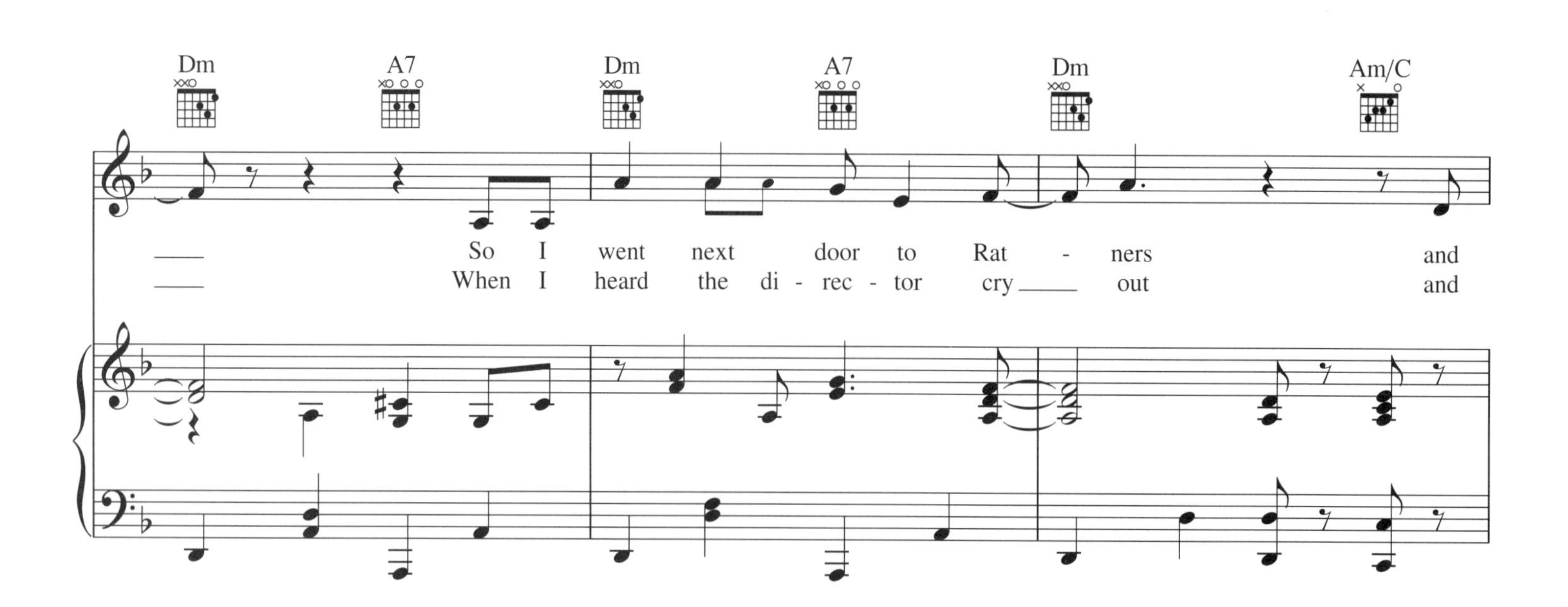
Dm
A7
Dm
A7
Dm
Am/C
So I went next door to Rat - ners and
When I heard the di - rec - tor cry out and

B♭7 A7♯5 Dm Em7 Ddim/F D/F♯ Gm7 C7
asked for a but - tered roll. The wait - ress sug - gest - ed a ba -
fall flat on his face. He went splat, not crunch.
F(add2) F Gm7(add4) C7 F(add2) F
- gel or a bi - al - i with a smear. She
You know I kind of had a hunch, so I
Gm7(add4) C7 F(add2) F/D F(add2)/G C7
said, "En - joy, don't fi - na - gle. Try it, you'll like it dear."
took a look and I was right; his face was in his lunch
F B♭sus2 B♭ B♭maj7 B♭6
She brought me
which con - sist - ed of
pink fish on a big stale

F(add2) F/C Fmaj7 F6/C C7sus
dough - nut with a glob of cream cheese
C7 F Gm7 A♭dim7 F/A
sit - ting on the side.
What is this
They were all eat - ing
B♭(add2) B♭/F B♭maj7 B♭6/F F(add2) F
pink fish? Am I sup - posed to eat this?
pink fish? It made me go nuts.
Fmaj7 F6/C C7sus C7
You did - n't e - ven heat this. I think it's still a -
I may have no guts, but I've got my

1
Dm
A7
Dm
Am/C
B♭
A7
live.
2
Dm
A7
Dm
Am/C
Then I
pride.
B♭
A7
B7
Em
B7
My
pas - tor came to vis -
3

Em B7 Em B7 Em B7
it; I made grits and chick - en fried steak.
Em B7 Em Bm/D C7 B7
Some - thing was wrong; I said, "Fa - ther, what is it?" He said, "Son, I need a
Em E/G♯ Am7 D7 G(add2) G
break! Take me to a Jew - ish del - i for a
Csus2/A D7 G(add2) G Csus2/A D7
3fr
corn beef and a knish. I may have a Tex - as bel -

G(add2) G Am7 B
Freely
-ly, but I want a New York Cit-y dish." Well, they
E C7 B7 Em
tell me that I faint-ed; I guess I could have passed for dead.
C7 B7 Em Em/D C♯m7♭5 Cmaj7 Em/A B7
I cried, "Oh Lord, please send a sign." He sent his son in-
Slightly slower
Em C F♯m7♭5/C D5/B G5/B
stead. And I dreamt I was fol-low-ing Je-sus and the

C
F♯m7♭5/C
3fr
D5/B
2fr
G5/B
C
F♯m7♭5/C
3fr
peo - ple were com - ing in droves. He said, "Try what my dad - dy hath
D5/B
2fr
Em7
Am7
D7
G
made to please us," and he took out the fish - es and the loaves.
A tempo
C(add2)
C
Cmaj7
C6
He was pass - ing out pink fish on big stale
G(add2)
G
Gmaj7
G6
D7sus
dough - nuts with globs of cream cheese

D7
G
Am7
B♭dim7
G/B
sit - ting on the side.
So I ate
C
Cmaj7
C6
C
G
Gmaj7
pink fish
and it made me go nuts.
G6
G
D7sus
D7
No ifs, ands, o' buts,
I swal - lowed my
Deliberately
G
C
D7
G
B+
C
pride.
A - maz - ing Grace, how sweet the
rit.

Freely
G
D7
taste that made a mensch of me.
Csus2/E
Fm6
D/F#
I once was lost but I found my
a tempo
Em
C#m7b5
A7
G/D
C/D
D7
pride. 'Cause I fixed my pink fish south - ern
G
G/F
C/E
Eb7
D7#5
G
fried.
Spoken: Good yun tov y'all!
L.H.

A PLACE CALLED HOME

from A CHRISTMAS CAROL

Music by ALAN MENKEN
Lyrics by LYNN AHRENS

Fmaj7
C(add9)/E
C/E
G/A
Am
home, full of love and fam - i -
D7sus
D7
Fmaj7
C/E
Em
Am
B♭
F/G
ly, and I'm there at the door watch-ing you come home to
dim.
C
Csus
3 fr
C
F
Dm9
G
me. Through the years,
mf
moving along
G7/F
C(add9)/E
Am
I'll re - call this day, in your

C/D
D9
4 fr
Dm/G
Em/G
arms, when I fin - 'lly found my
rall.
G7sus
C
Fmaj7
G9
way to a place called home, and a life with
a tempo
C(add9)
F6
G7
C(add9)/E
you, where the days are long and the love is
Am
D7sus
D9
4 fr
B♭
F/G
strong and the dreams are true. Just a place called

Fmaj7
C/E
G/A
Am
D7sus
D7
home you and I will al - ways see. In the
Fmaj7
C/E
Em
Am
B♭
F/G
Am
C/G
dark of the night let your heart come home to me, to the
p
Fmaj7
C/E
Em
Am
B♭
F/G
C
Csus
3 fr
C
F
Dm9
place in my heart where you're al - ways home with me. Through the
rall.
a tempo
f
G
G7/F
C(add9)/E
years I'll re - call this day,
with emotion

Am
C/D
D9
4 fr
in your arms,
when I fin - 'lly
dim.
Dm/G
Em/G
G7sus
Em/G
G7sus
C
found my way to a place called home,
rall.
molto rit.
a tempo
Fmaj7
F6
G9
C(add9)
F
F6
G7
and a life with you,
where the days are
C(add9)/E
Am
D7sus
B♭
long and the love is strong and the dreams are true.

F/G
Fmaj7
C(add9)/E
Just a place called home that my heart will
G/A
Am
D7sus
D7
Fmaj7
C/E
al - ways see. In the dark of the night let your
rall.
tenderly
Slower, freely
Em
Am
B♭
F/G
Am
C/G
Fmaj7
C/E
heart come home to me, to the place in my heart where you're
mp
Em
Am
B♭
F/G
C
Csus
3 fr
C
G7sus
C
al - ways home with me.
molto rit.
8vb

PROUD OF YOUR BOY

Music by ALAN MENKEN
Lyrics by HOWARD ASHMAN

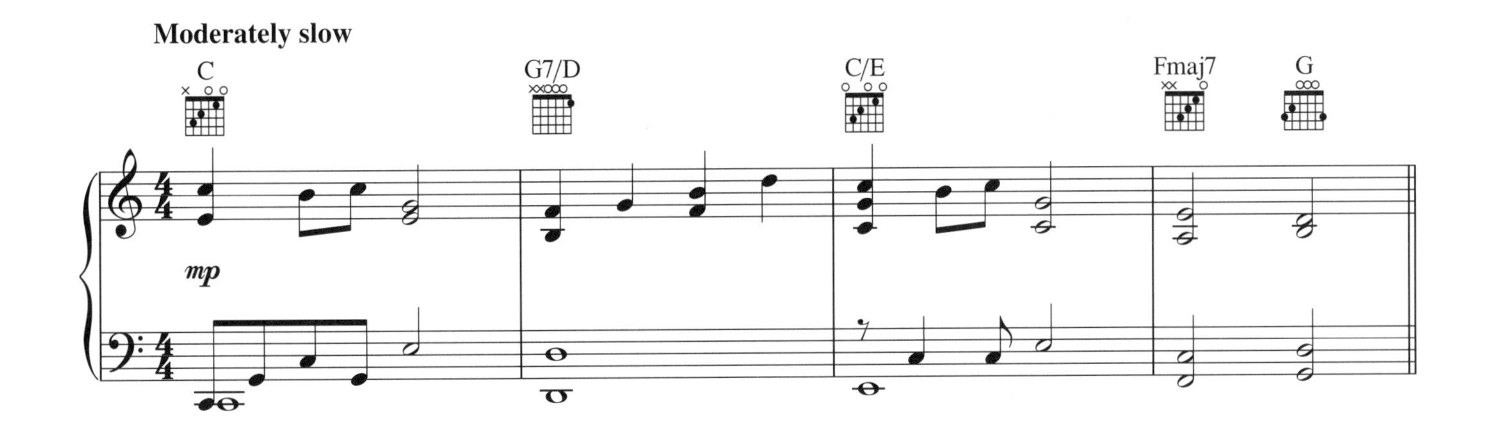

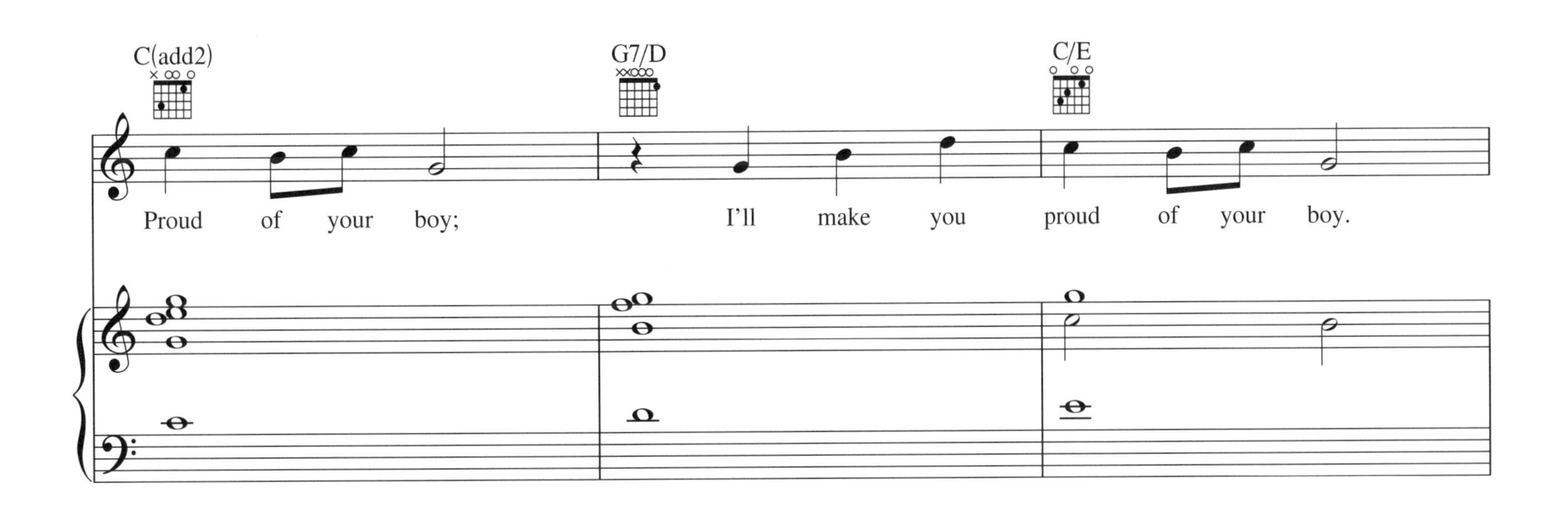

G7sus/D
G7sus
G7
Am
prise. I've wast - ed time,
E/G♯
Am
F♯m7♭5
Fdim
I've wast - ed me. So say I'm
C(add2)/E
C/E
Am7
D7sus
D7
B♭(add2)
slow for my age, a late bloom - er, o - kay, I a - gree
F/G
G7
C
G7/D
that I've been one rot - ten kid. Some son, some

C/E
Fmaj7
G7sus
G7
Am
Em/G
pride and some joy. But I'll get o - ver these lous - in' up,
Fmaj7
C(add2)/E
C/E
D7sus
D7
mess - in' up, screw - in' up times. You'll see, Ma,
Fmaj7
C(add2)/E
Am
now comes the bet - ter part. Some-one's gon - na make good, cross his stu - pid heart,
D7sus
D7
Dm7
Csus2/E
F/G
make good and fi - nal - ly make you proud of your

C
G7/D
C/E
Fmaj7
G
boy.
Più mosso
F
G/F
Tell me that I've been a louse and a loaf - er; you won't get a fight here, no
C(add2)/E
C/E
E♭
F/E♭
ma'am. Say I'm a gold - brick, a goof - off, no good, but that could - n't be all that I
Dm7
B♭/D
Gm9sus
Gm
C7sus
C7
3fr
am. Wa - ter flows un - der the bridge; let it pass, let it

F
Am
go.
There's no good rea - son that
D7sus
D7
Dm7
F/G
G
you should be - lieve me, not yet, I know but...
rit.
Tempo primo
C
G7/D
C/E
Some - day and soon, I'll make you proud of your boy.
Fmaj7
G7
Am
Em/G
Fmaj7
Em7
Though I can't make my - self tall - er or smart - er or hand - some or

D7sus
D7
Fmaj7
wise, I'll do my best, what else can I do?
Csus2/E
C/E
Am
D7sus
D7
Since I was - n't born per - fect like Dad or you, Mom, I will
p
rit.
A tempo
Dm
C/E
F/G
C
G7/D
try to, try hard to make you proud of your boy.
C/E
Fmaj7
G6
C
rit.
L.H.

SAILING ON

Music by ALAN MENKEN
Lyrics by DEAN PITCHFORD

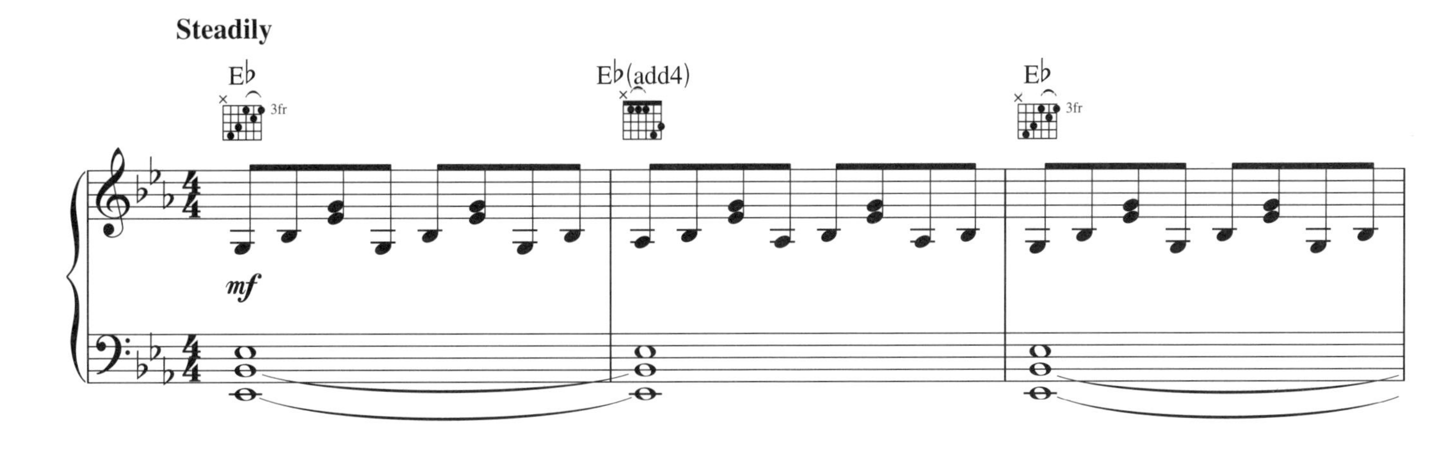

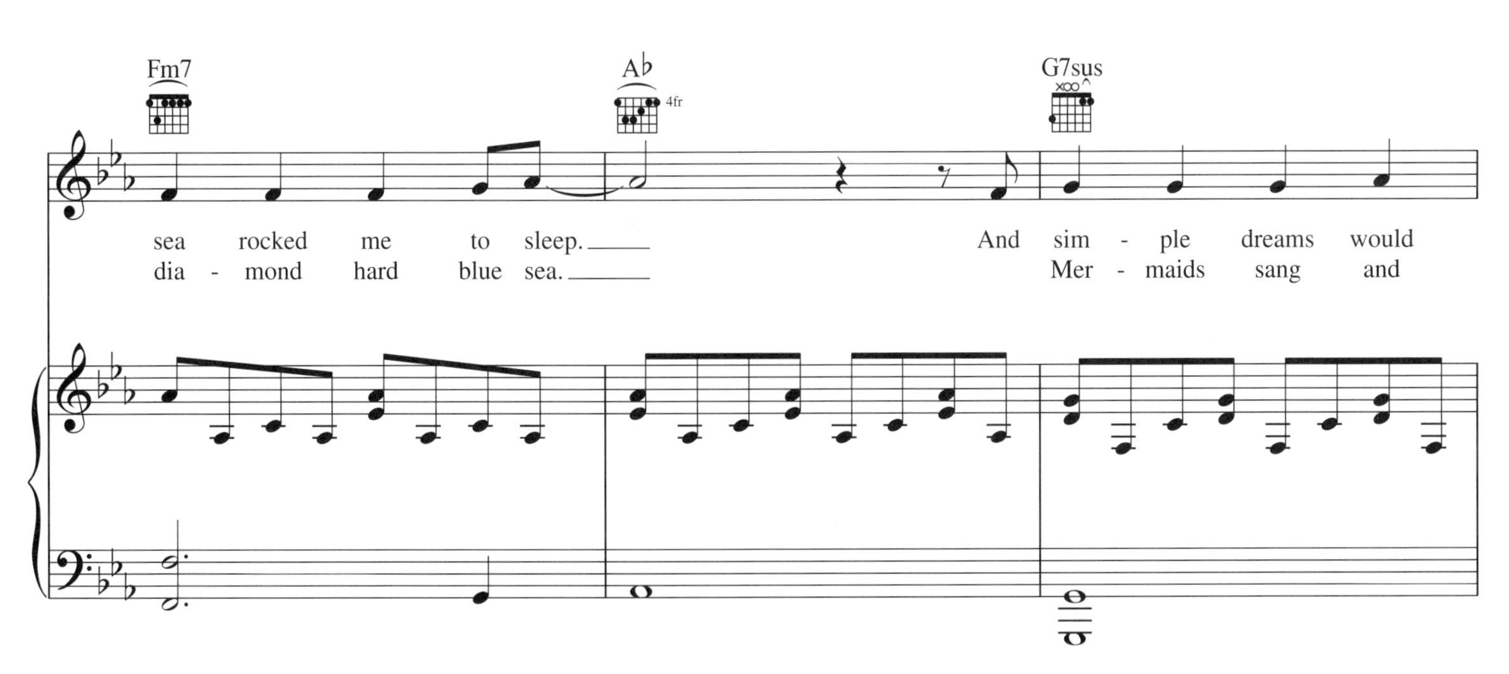

G7
G7/C
Cm/B♭
8fr
float to me like bub - bles from the deep. And
fly - ing fish would dance on air for me. I
Fm7
Gm7
A♭(add2)
4fr
sleep was like some o - pi - um I smoked on for - eign
made it home by sun - rise as day - light filled the
Am7♭5
E♭/B♭
6fr
shores. And dol - phins saw me safe - ly on as my
air. My face was wet with brine and foam and
E♭sus/B♭
6fr
B♭7
A♭
4fr
heart - strings pulled the oars. (1.,2.) And the ship was my
sand spilled from my hair. (D.S.) ship is my

B♭/A♭
A♭
B♭/A♭
bed and the waves were my pil - low. And the
bed and the waves are my pil - low. And the
Gm7
Cm7
Gm7
dark sky breathed and the sheets used to bil -
dark sky breathes and the sheets they all bil -
Cm7
Fm7
E♭sus/B♭
B♭
- low. And I'd go sail - ing on,
- low. And I go sail - ing on,
Gm7
Cm7
Fm7
sail - ing on. I'd go sail - ing
sail - ing on. I go sail - ing

To Coda
Ebsus/Bb
Bb7
Eb
Ab/Eb
on my dreams.
on my
Eb
Ab/Eb
Eb
dreams.
Ebsus
Abmaj7
The north - wind took me to
Gm7(add2)
Cm7
God knows where. O - ceans un -

F7sus
F7
A♭/B♭
4fr
Fm7
chart - ed,
drunk with salt air.
A♭/B♭
4fr
Cm
3fr
Gm7
ff
Cm/G
3fr
Fm
pp
A♭/B♭
4fr
B♭6

A♭/B♭
4fr
E♭sus/B♭
6fr
B♭
Cm
3fr
And ev - 'ry now and then I feel the
Fm
G7sus
need to take to sea,
give my - self to whin -

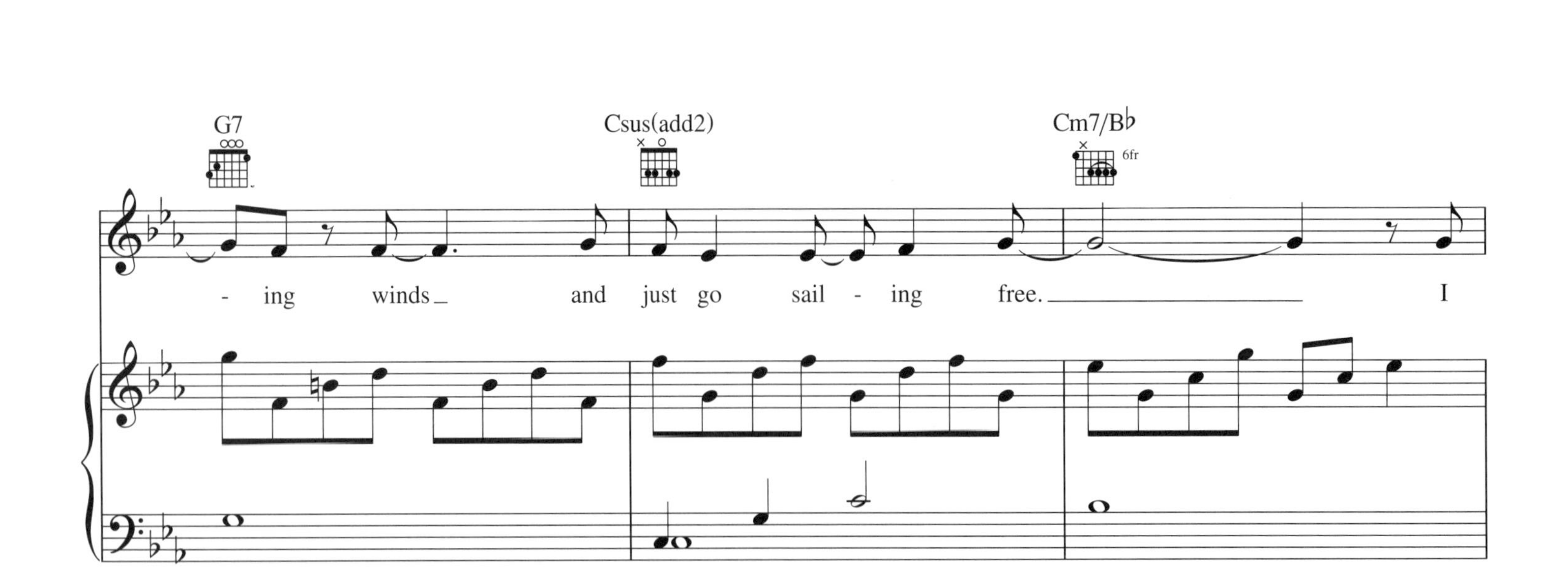
G7
Csus(add2)
Cm7/B♭
6fr
- ing winds and just go sail - ing free.
I

Fm7
E♭sus2/G
E♭/G
A♭(add2)
only need to lay me down, breathe so mild and
Am7♭5
E♭/B♭
then the ocean's rhythms sweep
E♭sus/B♭
B♭7
D.S. al Coda
me up and I'm a child again. And the
CODA
E♭
E♭sus
E♭
Fm7
dreams. Sailing on,

B♭7
Gm7
Cm7
3fr
sail - ing on, I go
Fm7
E♭sus/B♭
6fr
sail - ing on my
rit.
E♭
3fr
E♭(add4)
E♭
3fr
dreams.
a tempo
rit.
E♭(add4)
E♭
3fr

SANTA FE
from Walt Disney's NEWSIES

Lyrics by JACK FELDMAN
Music by ALAN MENKEN

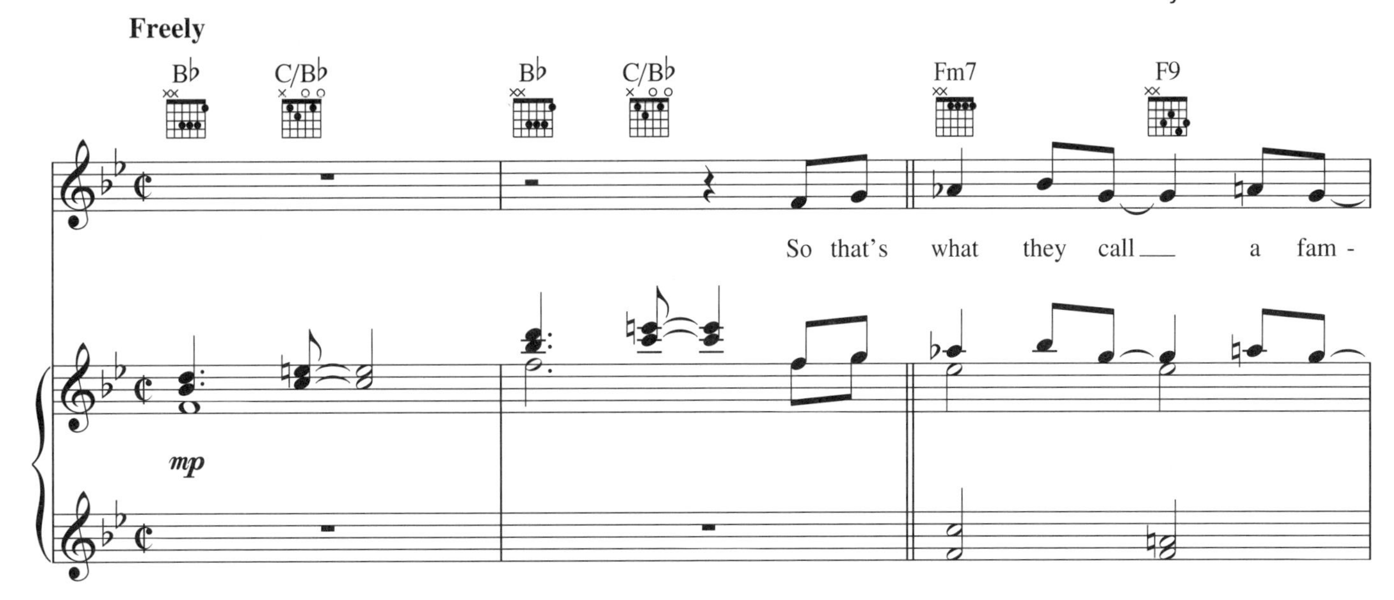

B♭
C/B♭
Fm7
F9
B♭(add9)
6fr
B♭
So you ain't got an - y fam - 'ly.
Well, who
Fm7
F9
B♭(add9)
6fr
Gm7
B♭/C
said you need - ed one?
Ain't ya glad no - bod - y's
C7
A♭(add9)
6fr
Fsus
F
wait - in' up for you?
When I
B♭
Gm
3fr
E♭
3fr
F
dream on my own
I'm a - lone but I ain't

E♭/B♭
B♭
F/A
D/F♯
Gsus
Gm
Gm/F
Dm/F
lone - ly. For a dream - er, night's the on - ly time of day.
E♭
B♭/D
Cm7
F7
When the cit - y's fi - n'ly sleep -
Dm7
Gm7
Cm7
F7
Dm7
Gm7
- in' all my thoughts be - gin to stray and I'm
D♭maj7
A♭maj7
Gm7
C7sus
C7
F7sus
on the train that's bound for San - ta Fe.

B♭
Gm
3fr
And I'm free like the wind, like I'm
E♭
3fr
F
F9
E♭/B♭
B♭
F/A
D/F♯
gon - na live for - ev - er. It's a feel - ing time can
Gsus
Gm
3fr
Gm/F
E♭
3fr
B♭/D
nev - er take a - way. All I
F7sus/C
3fr
F7
B♭(add9)/D
B♭/D
E♭maj7
3fr
F7
need's a few more dol - lars and I'm out - ta here to stay.

D7sus
D7
Cm9
F7sus
3fr
F7
B♭
C/B♭
Dreams come true. Yes, they do in San - ta Fe.
accel.
Somewhat faster
B♭
C/B♭
B♭
E♭
F/E♭
E♭
F/E♭
B♭
B♭(add9)
6fr
Where does it say you got - ta live and die here?
Where does it say a guy can't catch a break?
B♭/A♭
Gm7
Why should you on - ly take what you're giv - en? Why should you spend your
accel.

E♭m/G♭
Gm9
E♭maj9
whole life liv - in' trapped where there ain't no fu - ture. E - ven at sev - en -
D7♭9
Gm9
E♭maj9
teen break - in' your back for some - one else - 's sake.
A♭(add9)
A♭
Am7
If the life don't seem to suit ya, how 'bout a change of
D7
Gm
Gm/F
F/G
scene far from the lous - y head - lines and the dead - lines in be -

Broadly
F/G G7 F C Am
tween. San - ta Fe, are you there? Do you
accel.
F G G9 F/C C G E7/G♯ Asus Am Am/G
swear you won't for - get me? If I found you would you let me come and
F C/E Dm7 G7 C(add9)/E C/E
stay? I ain't get - tin' an - y young - er. And be -
Fmaj7 G7sus G7 E7sus E7 Dm11 G7sus G7
fore my dy - in' day I want space, not just air. Let 'em

C
Em7/B
Am
Cmaj7/G
Dm11
3fr
laugh in my face, I don't care. Save a place I'll be
rall.
F/G
Freely
C
D/C
C
D/C
Gm7
G9
there. So that's what they call a fam-
C(add9)
C
Gm7
G9
C(add9)
Am7
Dm9
3fr
-'ly. Ain't you glad you ain't that way? Ain't you glad you got a
G7sus
G7
C
D/C
C
D/C
C
dream called San - ta Fe?

SOMEDAY

from Walt Disney's THE HUNCHBACK OF NOTRE DAME

Music by ALAN MENKEN
Lyrics by STEPHEN SCHWARTZ

D♭(add2)
A♭/C
A♭/E♭
E♭sus
E♭7
live and let live.
A♭
Cm/G
D♭/F
Cm/E♭
Some - day life will be fair - er, need will be
B♭m(add2)/D♭
A♭/C
B♭m7(add4)
E♭7
rar - er, greed will not pay.
B♭m7
E♭/G
E♭7/G
D♭6/A♭
A♭
D♭
God - speed this bright mil - len - ni - um

B♭m6/F
Fm
B♭m
E♭7/D♭
D♭
E♭6
E♭
A♭
Cm/G
on its way. Let it come some - day.
D♭/F
Cm/E♭
B♭m/D♭
A♭/C
F7sus
F7
cresc.
rall.
Broadly
B♭
Dm/A
Dm7/A
E♭/G
Dm/F
Some - day our fight will be won then, we'll stand in the
Cm/E♭
B♭/D
Cm7
Cm7(add4)
F7sus
F7
sun then, that bright af - ter - noon.

Cm
F
Eb6/Bb
Bb
Eb(add9)
Till then, on days when the sun is gone,
Cm6/G
Gm
Cm7
F/Eb
Eb
Ebmaj7/F
F#dim7
Gm
Gm7/F
we'll hang on, wish up - on the moon.
Slower
Cm
Bb/D
Eb6
Eb6/F
Eb/F
Ebmaj7/F
F7
Bb
Ebm6/Bb
Change will come one day, some - day soon.
p sub.
a tempo
Bb
Ebm6/Bb
Bb
Ebm6/Bb
Bb
rit.

SOMEWHERE THAT'S GREEN

Music by ALAN MENKEN
Lyrics by HOWARD ASHMAN

F/G G7 F/C C C♯m7♭5
4fr
To Coda
dry - er and an i - ron - ing ma - chine in a
fur - ni - ture to keep it neat and clean in the
Bet - ter Homes and Gar - dens mag - a - zine.
G/D D7sus D7 G C/G D/G 1 G C/G D7sus2
tract house that we share some - where that's green. He
Pine - Sol scent - ed air some - where that's green.
2 G E♭ F/E♭
Be - tween our fro - zen din - ner and our
cresc.
mf
G/D D7 G Em B/D♯
bed - time, nine fif - teen, we snug - gle watch - in' Lu -

G/D
A7/C♯
A7
D
A7/C♯
D7
D.S. al Coda
- cy on our big, e - nor - mous twelve - inch screen. I'm
rit.
CODA
C♯m7♭5
4fr
G/D
Far from Skid Row,
freely
D7sus
I dream we'll go some - where that's
8va
G
C/G
D/G
G
C/G
D/G
G
C/G
D/G
G
green.
a tempo
8va

TAKE CARE OF MY HEART

Music by ALAN MENKEN
Lyrics by JACK FELDMAN

F♯m11
B7sus
B7
E/G♯
bet - ter?
What else can I give you but a kiss,
and
D9
G
D/G
G6
D/G
G
this?
Wher - ev - er I wan - der, my heart will be stay - ing with
car - riage is wait - ing, and peo - ple are count - ing on
Csus2
C
G
C6
Am7
you.
What - ev - er you do,
you,
but I need you too.
Original Tempo
D7sus
D7
G
Am/G
G
Am/G
take care of my heart.
The
Take care of my heart.
The

G D/G G6 D/G G Csus2 C Cmaj7
3fr
long - er my jour - ney, the strong - er I need __ you to be.
long - er your jour - ney, the strong - er I prom - ise to be.
C6 C G/B Am7 D7sus D
Keep smil - ing for me; take care of my
Just come back to me; take care of my
3
G Am/G G C
heart. Some - times the nights __ may __ be lone -
heart. I know I'm good __ at __ pre - tend -
G/B Am7 D7sus D7 Am/G G D/G G
- ly but noth - ing's as bad __ as it seems, __ for you're
- ing, but this time the sto - ry's too sad, __ so I'll

C Bm Em Fsus2 F
my one and on - ly and you're safe in - side my dreams.
skip to the end - ing an - y time I'm feel - ing
D9(no3rd) D D7/F♯ G D/G G6 D/G G
And we'll be to - geth - er, though I may be o - ceans a -
bad. When we'll be to - geth - er for - ev - er, the way we are
Csus2 C Cmaj7 C6 Am
way, and some bright - er day
now, I still don't know how,
Am/D D7 Em Em/D
I'll hold you a - gain. Take care of my
I still don't know when, but noth - ing on

1
C
D7sus
D7
G
Am/G
G
Am/G
heart 'til then.
G
Am/G
G
Am7
D7sus
2
Csus2
3fr
C
Cmaj9
C6
The earth can keep us a-
3
3
Am7
Slower
D7sus
D
D7
part. Take care of my heart 'til
3
3
Original Tempo
G
Am
D7
G
Am
D7
G
Am
D7
G(add2)
then.

SUDDENLY SEYMOUR

Music by ALAN MENKEN
Words by HOWARD ASHMAN

Adim7
A
E7sus
A
Here, take my Klee - nex. Wipe that lip - stick a - way.
D/A
A
D/A
A
Show me your face, clean as the morn - in'. I
I'd meet a man and I'd fol - low him blind - ly.
Please un - der - stand that it's still strange and fright - 'nin'. For
Adim7
A
E7sus
A
know things were bad, but now they're o - kay.
He'd snap his fin - gers. Me, I'd say "sure".
los - ers like I've been it's so hard to say:
Bm7
A7/C♯
D
Sud - den - ly Sey - mour
Sud - den - ly Sey - mour
Sud - den - ly Sey - mour,
cresc.
mf

A/D
D
A/C♯
Bm7
A
is stand - in' be - side you.
is stand - in' be - side me.
he pur - i - fied me.
E/A
A
A/C♯
B/D♯
E
You don't need no make - up,
He don't give me or - ders.
Sud - den - ly Sey - mour
B/E
E
D
A/C♯
Bm7
A
don't have to pre - tend.
He don't con - de - scend.
showed me I can
A9sus/E
5fr
A
Bm7
A7/C♯
D
Sud - den - ly Sey - mour
Sud - den - ly Sey - mour
learn how to be more

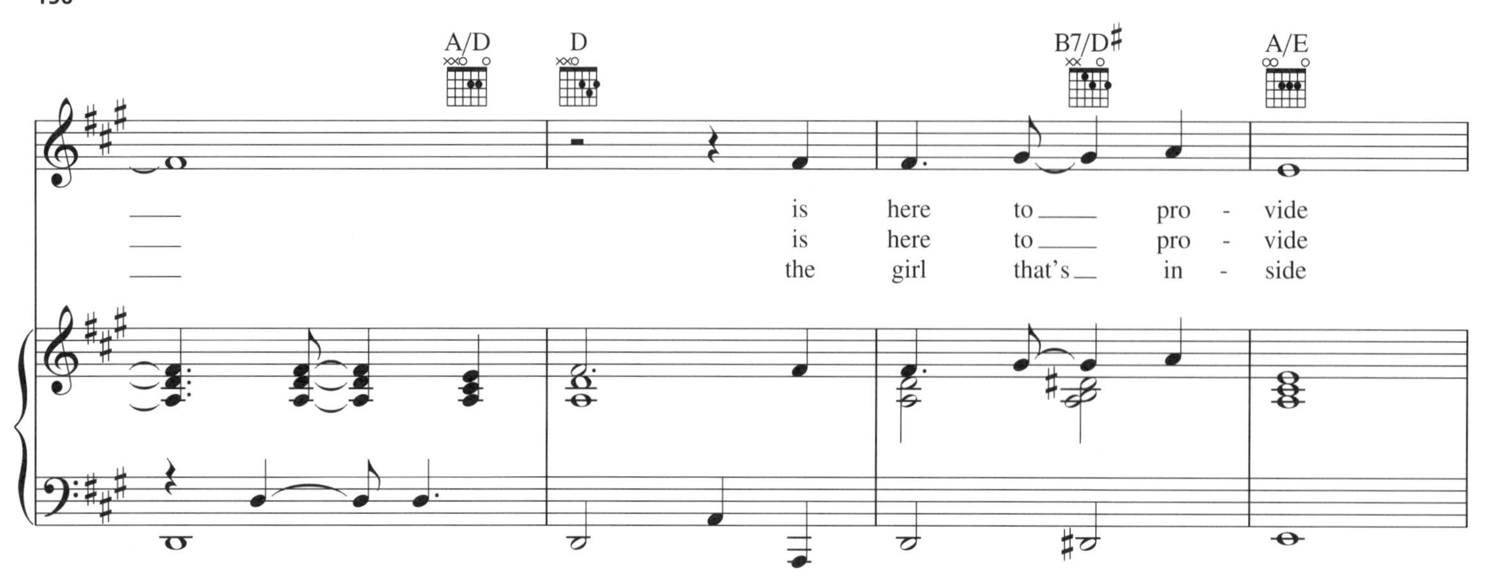
A/D
D
B7/D♯
A/E
is here to pro - vide
is here to pro - vide
the girl that's in - side

C♯7/E♯
F♯m
F♯m/E
To Coda
A/B
you sweet un - der -
me sweet un - der -
me. With sweet un - der -

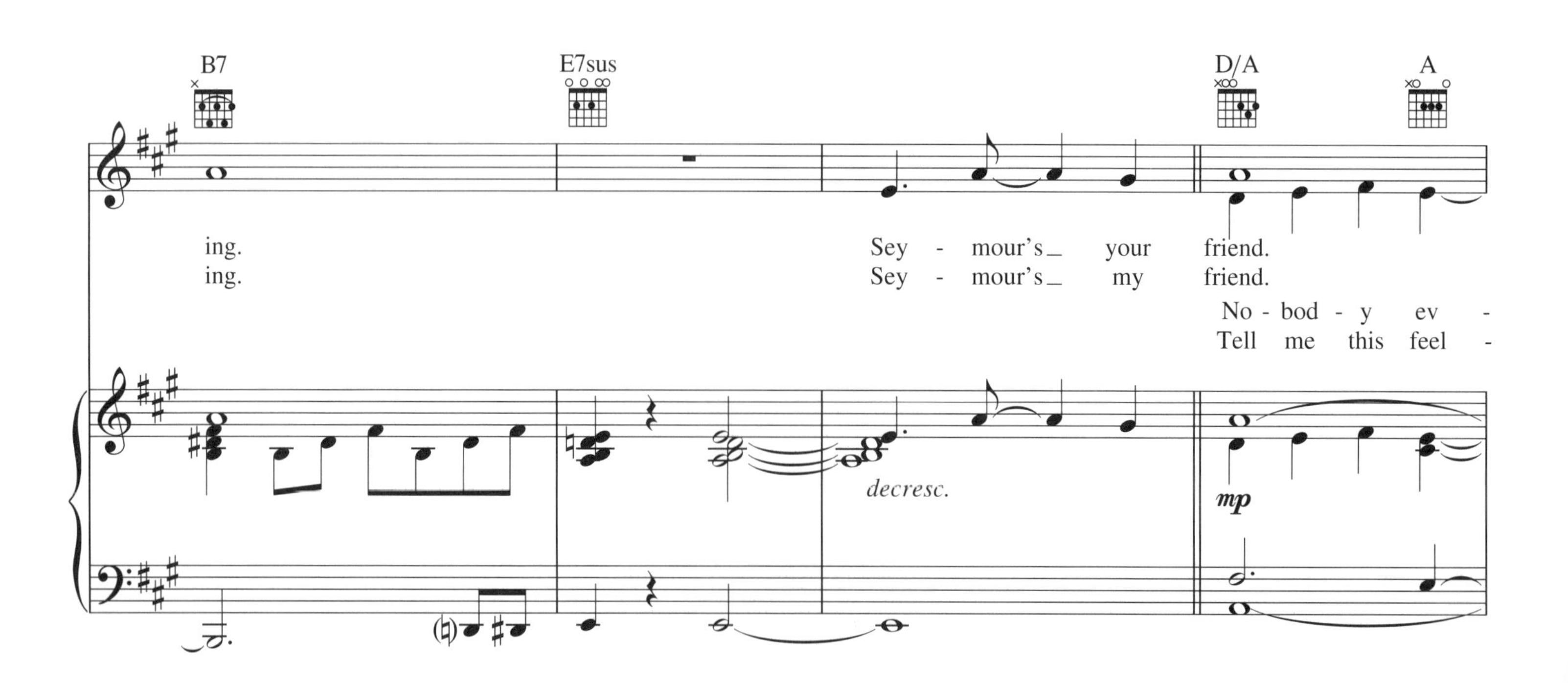
B7
E7sus
D/A
A
ing. Sey - mour's your friend.
ing. Sey - mour's my friend.
No - bod - y ev -
Tell me this feel -
decresc.
mp

D/A
A
-er treat-ed me kind-ly.
-in' lasts till for-ev-er.
Adim7
A
E7sus
A
Dad-dy left ear-ly. Ma-ma was poor.
Tell me the bad times are clean washed a-way.
1
2
D.S. al Coda
CODA
B7sus
2fr
stand-
B7
ing, with sweet un-der-

Dm
stand - ing, with sweet un - der -
A/E
E7sus
stand - ing, Sey - mour's my
A
B/A
man.
Bdim/A
A

THESE ARE THE GOOD TIMES

Music by ALAN MENKEN
Lyrics by TOM EYEN

Freely

G(add2) D7#5

So it don't look too good from here.

mf

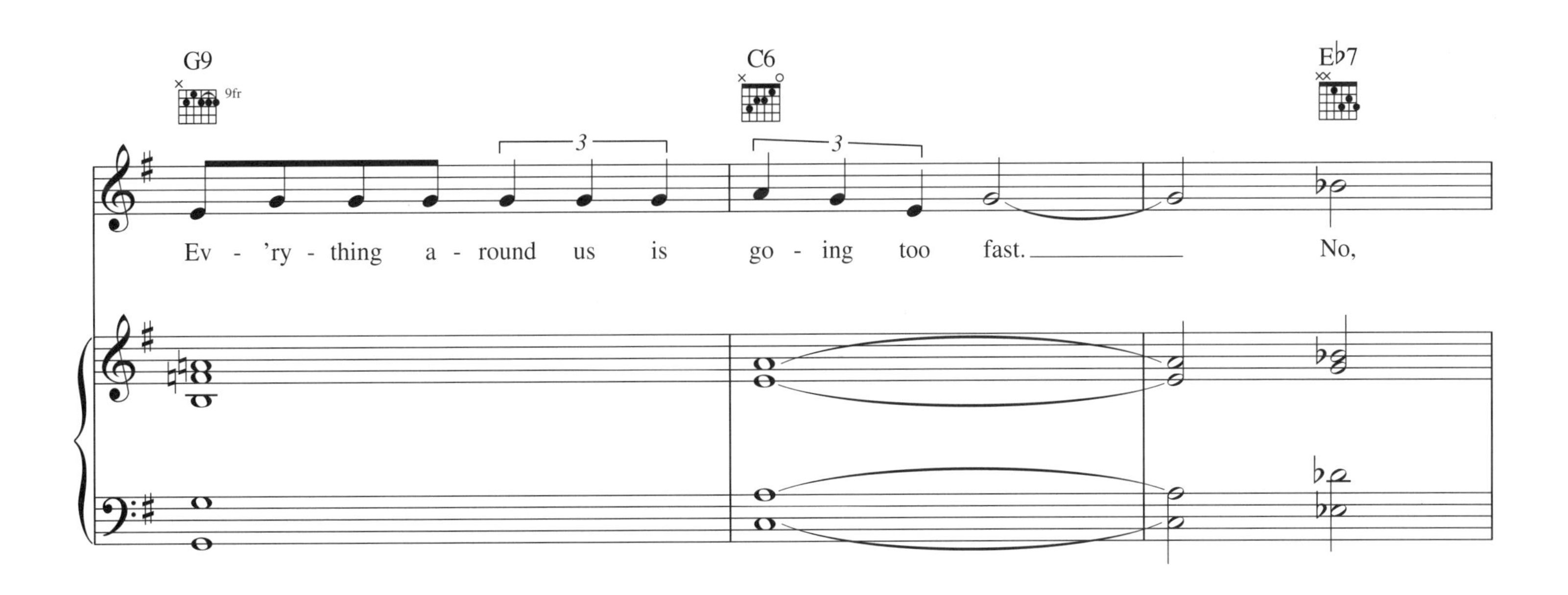

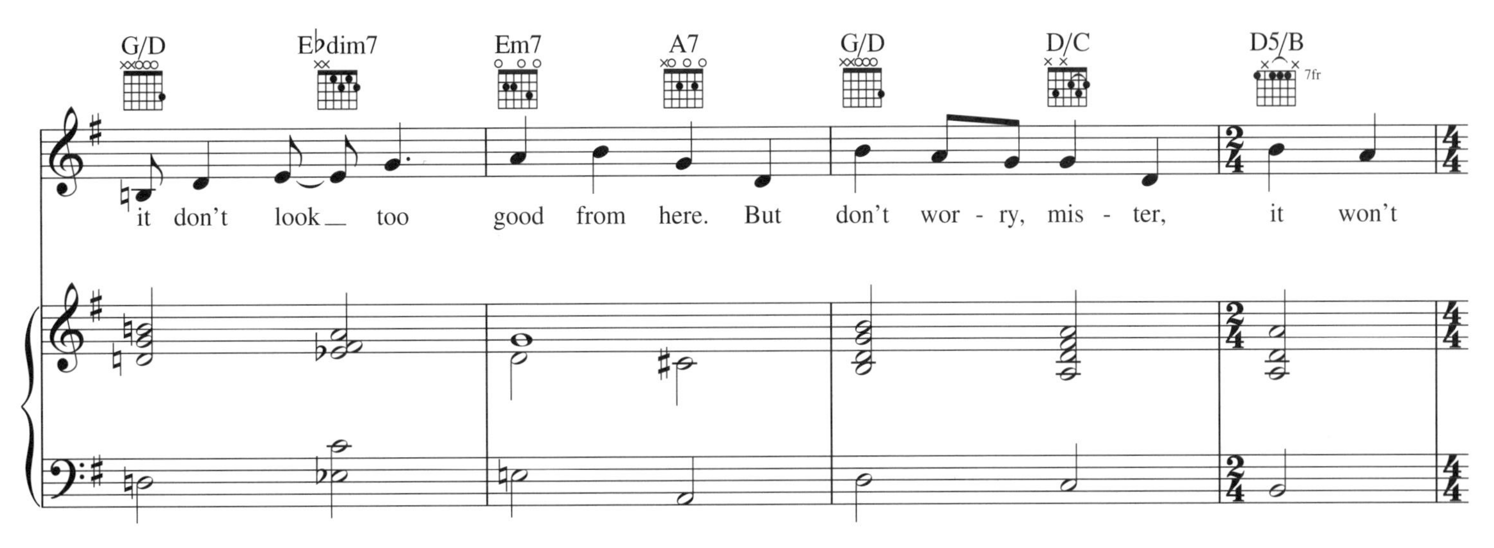

A7
G/B
C(add2)
C
Bm7
Gsus2/B
last. 'Cause we peo - ple to - day are blessed by a guid - ing
A7
D5/B
Cm6
A/C♯
G/D
E♭dim
Em7
star. Yes, look up, mis - ter;
Am7
Cmaj7/D
D7
With spirit
G(add2)
don't you know what times these are?
8va
Gsus/A
G(add2)/B
Gsus/A
Gsus/D

G(add2)
Gsus/A
Gsus/D
G(add2)/B
3fr
These are the good times.
These are the
E7
A7sus
A7
great times.
These are the best times there's
D7sus
D7
C/E
Fm
D7/F♯
ev - er gon - na be!
These are the
loco
D7sus/A
bright times.
These are the right times.

G(add2)/B
E7
G(add2)/A
A7
These are the great - est times we're ev -
D7sus
D7
G
- er gon - na see!
And
B
F♯7sus/C♯
F♯7sus
there's no tell - ing how hap - py we are now.
F♯5/D♯
G♯m7
4fr
F♯7sus/C♯
F♯7sus
We're much too bus - y laugh - ing to see how

D
Dmaj7
D6
Dmaj7
luck - y we are
and how
per - fect life can be.
And
Em
C♯m7♭5
G(add2)/A
Em7(add4)
look out the win - dow;
There's
noth - ing but good times
A7
C/D
D♭/E♭
as far as I can see.
A♭(add2)
E♭7sus/B♭
E♭7sus
A♭(add2)/C
These are the good years.
These are the

E♭7sus/B♭ E♭7sus Cm7 F9 A♭/B♭ B♭7
great years. These are the best years we're
E♭7sus E♭7 A♭sus/F G♭m6 E♭7/G A♭(add2)
ev - er gon - na hold! These are the
A♭sus/B♭ Cm7 A♭sus/B♭ E♭7sus
bright years. These are the right years.
Cm7 F7 A♭/B♭ B♭7/F D♭/E♭
These are the great - est years. They're great, they're

A♭
B♭m
E♭
right, they're bold!
C(add2)
And there's no tell - ing what's out
G7sus/D
G7sus
Em7
Am7
there be - fore us. We're gon - na make the fu -
G7sus/D
G7
E♭
Gm/B♭
ture a - dore us. How luck - y we are. And we

E♭6
Gm/B♭
Fm(add2)
Fm/C
don't have a care. And look out the win - dow;
Fm
Fm/E♭
Dm7♭5
Fm/C
A♭/B♭
B♭7
the storm has gone and a
D♭/E♭
D/E
E
D/E
E7
rain - bow's shin - ing there.
rit.
Slightly slower
A(add2)
E7sus/B
E7sus
Asus2/C♯
These are the good times. These are the

E7sus/B
E7sus
C♯m7
4fr
F♯7
A/B
B7/F♯
great times.
These are the best times there's
E7sus
E7
Gdim
E7/G♯
A
ev - er gon - na be.
These are the
E7sus/B
A/C♯
F♯m7
E7sus/B
E7sus
E7
bright years.
These are the right years.
C♯m7
4fr
F♯7
A/B
B7
D/E
C♯m/E
4fr
D/E
These are the great - est years:
nine - teen fif -

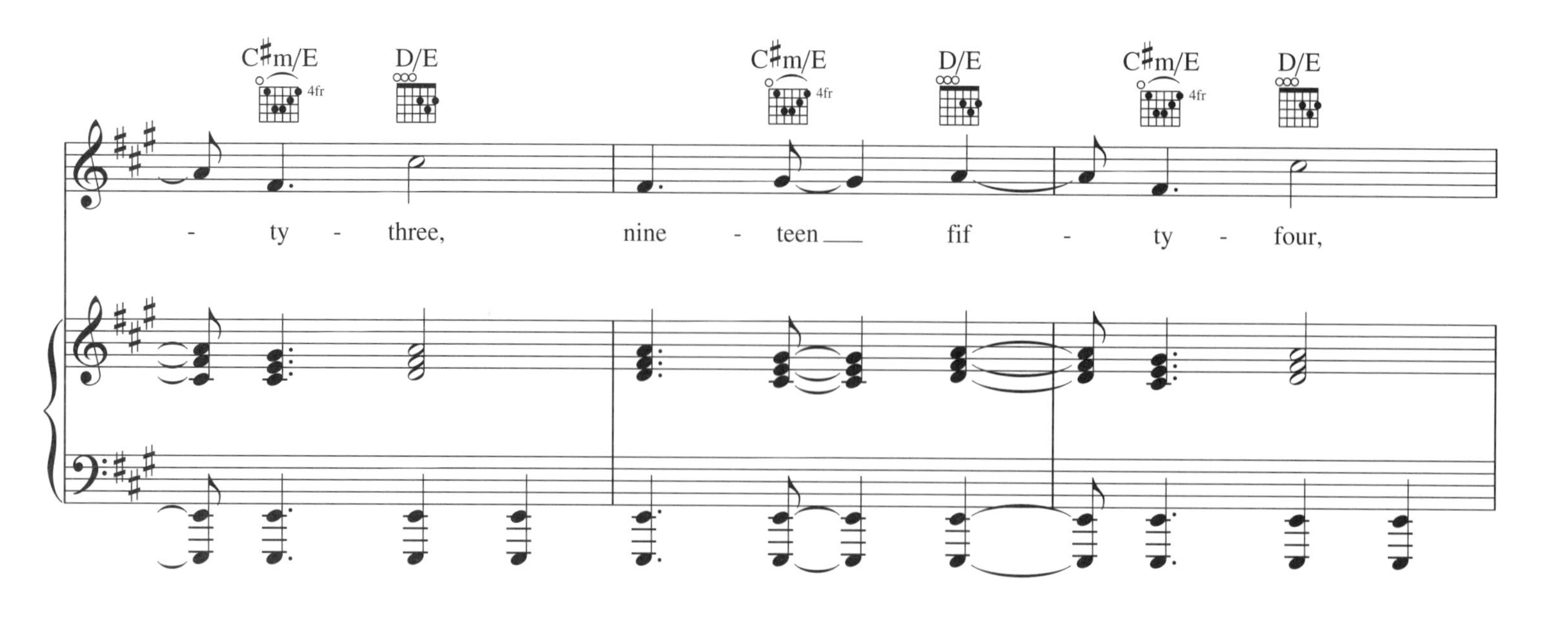
C♯m/E
D/E
C♯m/E
D/E
C♯m/E
D/E
4fr
- ty - three, nine - teen fif - ty - four,

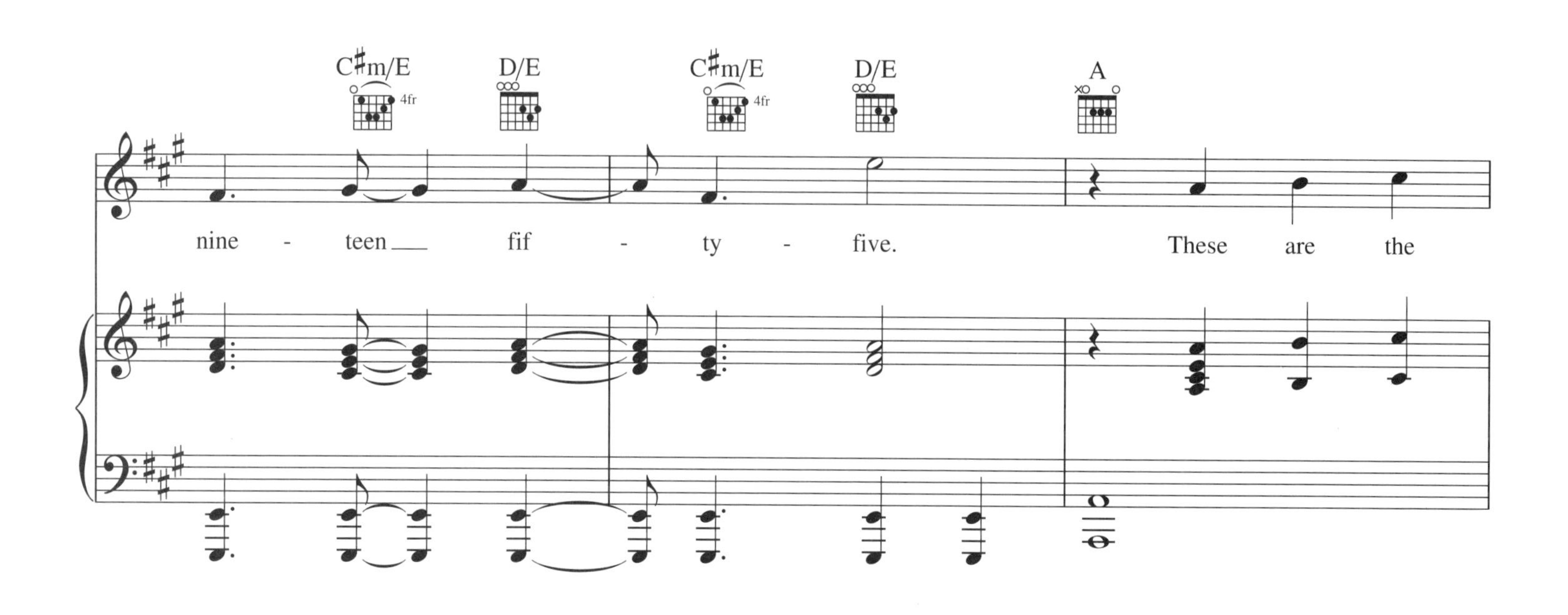
C♯m/E
D/E
C♯m/E
D/E
A
4fr
nine - teen fif - ty - five. These are the

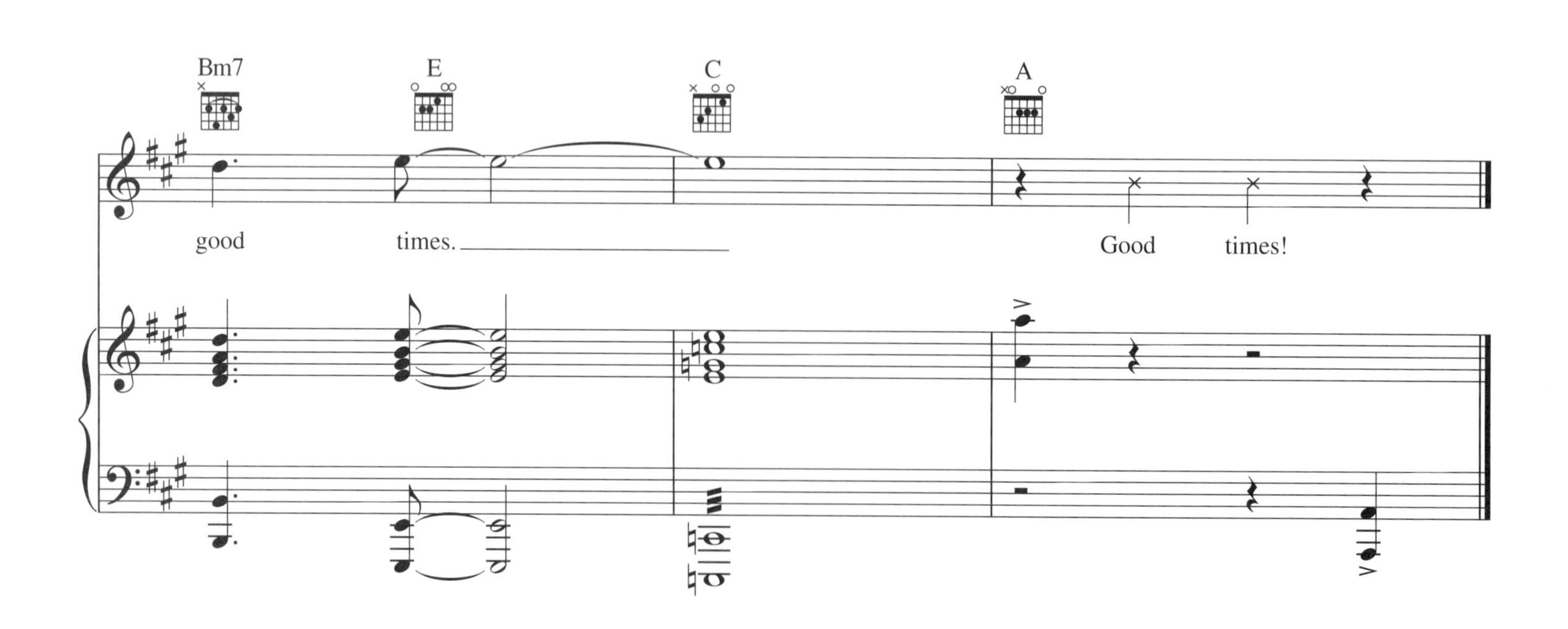
Bm7
E
C
A
good times. Good times!

THIS NEW JERUSALEM

Music by ALAN MENKEN
Lyrics by TIM RICE

E♭ A7sus A7 Dm
deeds of our an - ces - tors, their sup - pli - ca - tion and prayer. Nev - er
B♭maj7 Dm/A A7sus A7
once Los - ing their faith in their God through the years of de -
f
Warmly, in 4
D5 D Gm/D D Edim/D
spair. I am the blood of A - bra - ham The
poco rall.
D/F♯ G6 D/A A7sus D Gm/D D F♯7
seed of an im - mor - tal line Whose life was giv - en to his God Whose

Bm G6 D/A A7 D/F♯ G
promise to his God is mine And to this new Je -
Bm A7/C♯ D G A D/F♯ G A
ru - sa - lem Our fa - thers come at last
D/F♯ G Bm F♯m G(add2) Bm A/C♯
The sons of Ja - cob live a - gain The glo - ries of our sa - cred past
D G Bm A/C♯ D G A
Je - ru - sa - lem, Je - ru - sa - lem Though pa - lac - es may
mf

D/F♯
G
A
D/F♯
G
Bm
rise
With - in your walls, your dust your
F♯m
D/F♯
G(add9)
Em7
stones Are prize e - nough for
D(add2)/A
7fr
D/A
A7sus
A7
D
these con - tent - ed eyes.
I shall
p
Tempo Primo
B♭/D
E/D
Edim/D
3fr
build the Lord a tem - ple in this ho - ly
mf
3
3

Dm
B♭/D
E/D
town as we move to - ward one
Edim/D
3fr
F
F/E♭
na - tion and one sin - gle crown. Lest we should pre -
Dm7
B♭/D
E♭
3fr
A7sus
A7
tend our earth - ly a - chieve-ments are some-how the work of mere
Dm
Dm/C
B♭
Dm/A
man, this I know: God is the rea - son, at
f

A7sus
A7
D5
5fr
best we are part of His plan.
poco rall.
Warmly, in 4
D
Gm/D
D
Edim/D
3fr
D/F♯
G6
I am the blood of A - bra - ham The seed of an im -
mp
A6
A7sus
A7
D
Gm/D
D
F♯7
mor - tal line Whose life was giv - en to his God Whose
Bm
G6
A6
A
D
G
prom - ise to his God is mine And to this new Je -
mf

Bm
A7/C♯
D
G
D/F♯
G
A
ru - sa - lem Our fa - thers come at last
D/F♯
G
Bm
F♯m
G(add2)
The sons of Ja - cob live a - gain; the glo - ries of our
Bm
A/C♯
A
sa - cred past
poco rall.
Broader
F
B♭
Dm
C7
F
B♭
C/B♭
F/A
B♭
C
Je - ru - sa lem, Je - ru - sa - lem Though pa - lac - es may rise
ff

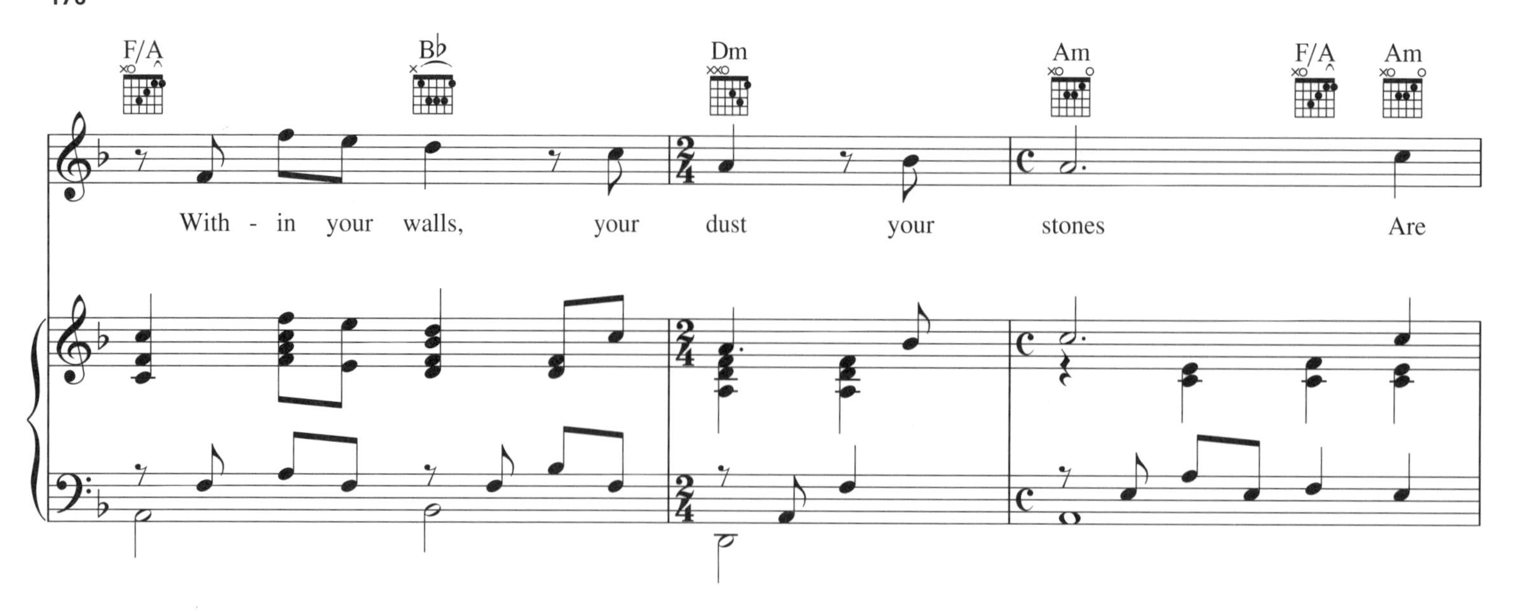
F/A
B♭
Dm
Am
F/A
Am
With - in your walls, your dust your stones Are

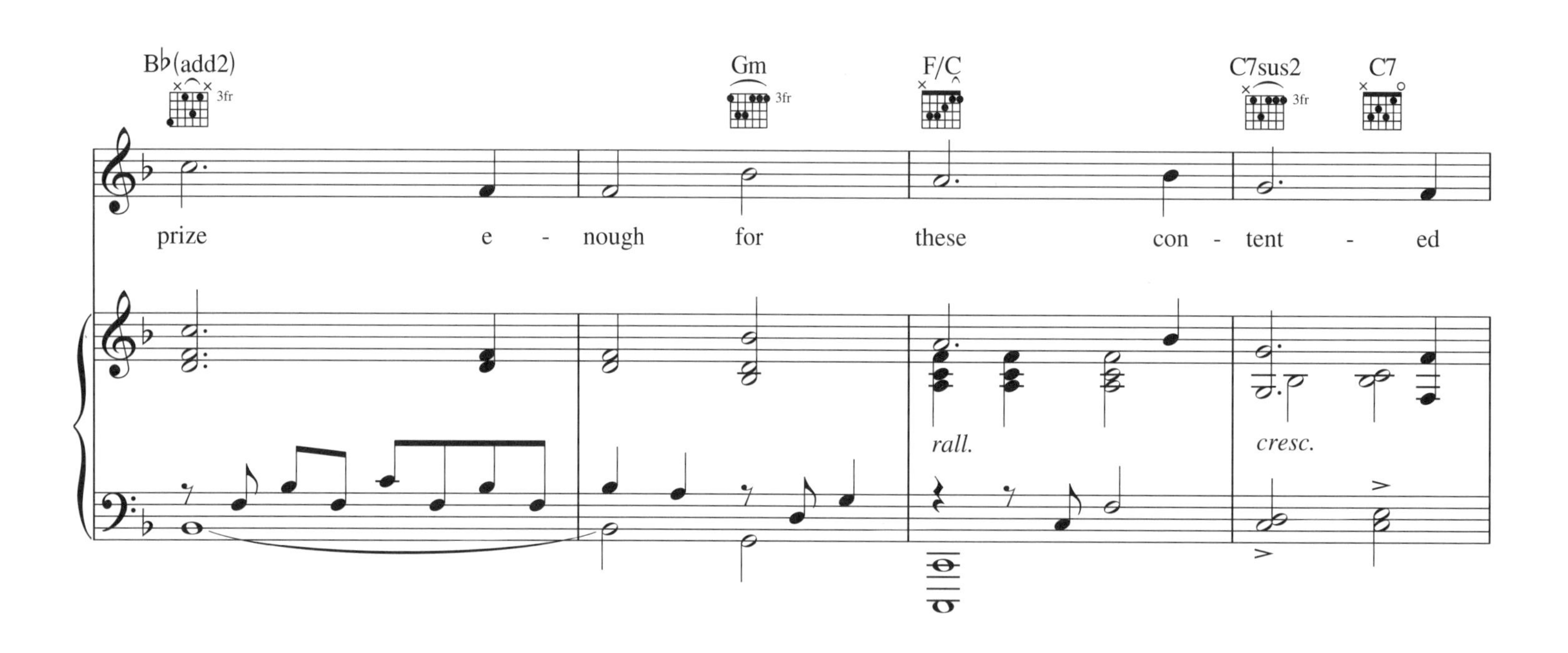
B♭(add2)
3fr
Gm
3fr
F/C
C7sus2
3fr
C7
prize e - nough for these con - tent - ed
rall.
cresc.

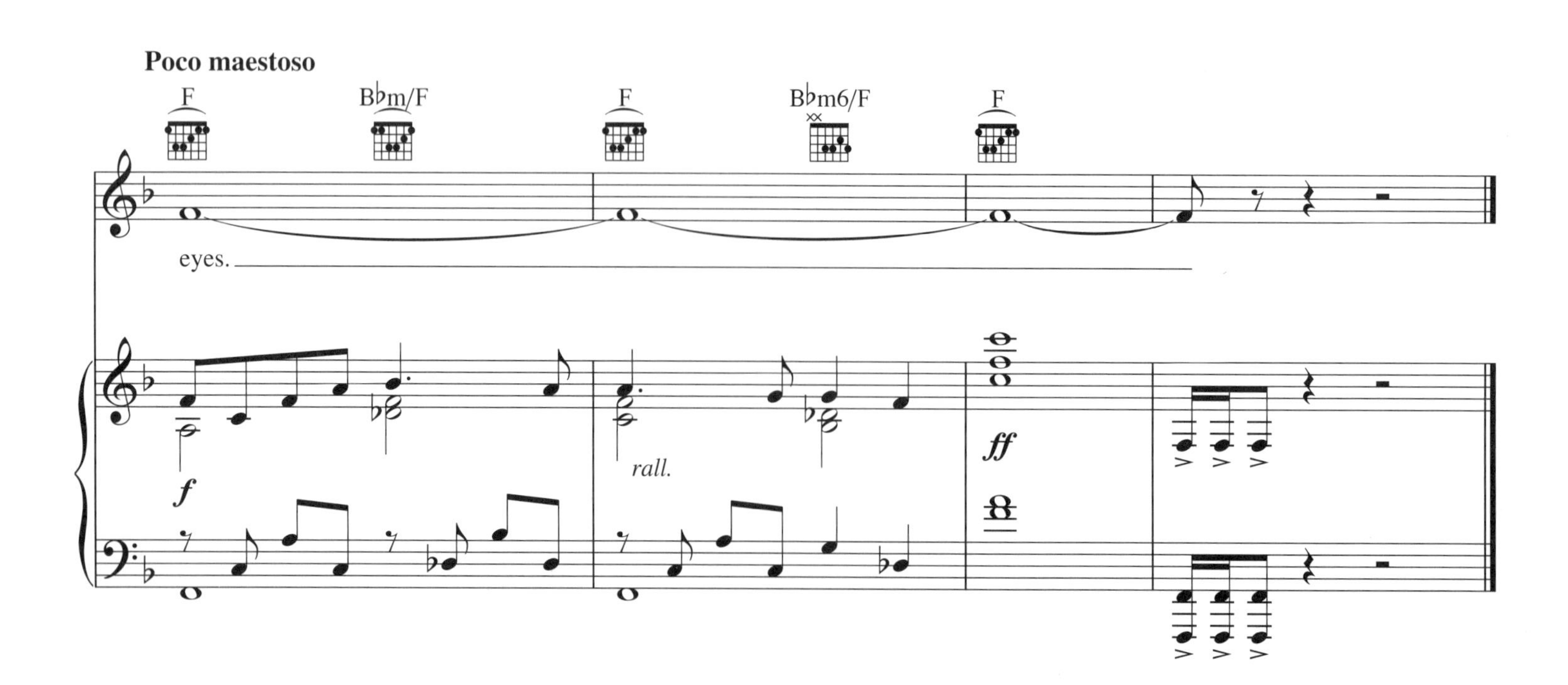
Poco maestoso
F
B♭m/F
F
B♭m6/F
F
eyes.
f
rall.
ff

WE'LL HAVE TOMORROW

Music by ALAN MENKEN
Lyrics by HOWARD ASHMAN

Dsus(add2)
5fr
Dm
A
this mess that I made.
Bb/C
G/A
3fr
A7
D
E9
Don't ask ques-tions to-night, it's touch and go.
D/F#
E9
Bb/C
A7sus
A7
No one ev-er got hurt by what they don't know.
D
E
D/F#
F
C
We'll have to-mor-row.

Am7
D
A/D
D
Trust me, it's true.
We'll have to-
F
C
Em7
D
A7sus
mor-row; we'll get through.
A
D
F
C
Am7
Clouds will be part-ed;
sun will shine
D
A/D
D
F
C
bright.
We'll have to-mor-row

Em7
D
B♭sus2
B♭
Asus
if we make it through to - night.
Slight pullback
A
F
A♭
E♭
E♭/C
We'll have a fam - 'ly, three kids or
F
A♭
E♭
four. Light in the win - dow;
Gm7
F
Dm7
C
G/C
C
F
Christ - mas wreath on the door. Ros - es are

A♭
E♭
E♭/C
F
C/F
red, love; wed - dings are white.
A♭
E♭
Gm7
F
We'll have to - mor - row if we
D♭sus
Csus
C
just get through to - night!
rit.
p
A tempo
Fsus(add2)
Fm(add2)
Fsus(add2)
Fm
C

Fsus(add2)
Fm(add2)
Fsus(add2)
Fm
Don't you be fright - ened, don't be a -
C
Fsus(add2)
Fm(add2)
fraid. If we see to - mor - row,
Fsus(add2)
Fm
C
we'll have it made.
cresc.
pf
ff

A WHOLE NEW WORLD

from Walt Disney's ALADDIN

Music by ALAN MENKEN
Lyrics by TIM RICE

D
I can o - pen your eyes, take you won - der by
G/B A/C♯ Em/G F♯7 F♯7/A♯ Bm Bm/A
won - der, o - ver, side - ways and un - der on a
G D A
mag - ic car - pet ride. A whole new world,
D A A7/C♯ D(add9) D
a new fan - tas - tic point of view. No one to

A/G
D/F♯
A/G
D/F♯
Bm7
2fr
E7sus
E7
tell us no or where to go or say we're on - ly dream -
G/A
A
D
ing. A whole new world, a daz - zling
A
A♯dim7
Bm
D7/A
A/G
D/F♯
place I nev - er knew. But when I'm way up here, it's
3
A/G
D/F♯
Bm7
2fr
E7sus
E7
C
A7sus
A7
crys - tal clear that now I'm in a whole new world with

D
F
you.
Un - be - liev - a - ble
B♭/D
C/E
sights,
in - de - scrib - a - ble
feel - ing.
Gm/B♭
A7sus
A7/C♯
Dm
Dm/C
B♭
Soar - ing, tum - bling, free - wheel - ing through an end - less dia - mond sky.
F
C
F
A whole new world,
a hun - dred

C
F
C/B♭
F/A
3
thou - sand things be - gin. I'm like a shoot - ing star, I've
C/B♭
F/A
Dm7
G7sus
G7
B♭/C
come so far; I can't go back. I'm in a whole new
C
F
C
C♯dim7
world with new ho - ri - zons to pur - sue.
Dm
F7/C
3fr
C/B♭
F/A
C/B♭
F/A
I'll chase them an - y - where. There's time to spare.

Dm7 G7sus G7 E♭ B♭/C C7 Dm
Let me share this whole new world with you.
F/C B♭(add9) F/A Gm7(add4)
A whole new world, that's where we'll be.
F/A B♭(add9) C7sus F
A thrill - ing chase, a won - d'rous place for you and me.
rit.
Ped.